Congressional
Research
Service

Tax Havens: International Tax Avoidance and Evasion

Jane G. Gravelle
Senior Specialist in Economic Policy

January 23, 2013

Congressional Research Service

7-5700

www.crs.gov

R40623

CRS Report for Congress —————

Prepared for Members and Committees of Congress

Summary

Recent actions by the Organization for Economic Cooperation and Development (OECD) and the G-20 industrialized nations have targeted tax haven countries, focusing primarily on evasion issues. The HIRE Act (P.L. 111-147) included a number of anti-evasion provisions, and P.L. 111-226 included foreign tax credit provisions. Some of these proposals, and some not adopted, are in the American Jobs and Closing Loopholes Act (H.R. 4213); the Stop Tax Haven Abuse Act (S. 506, H.R. 1265); draft proposals by the Senate Finance Committee; two other related bills, S. 386 and S. 569; the Bipartisan Tax Fairness and Simplification Act (S. 3018); and proposals by President Obama.

Multinational firms can artificially shift profits from high-tax to low-tax jurisdictions using a variety of techniques, such as shifting debt to high-tax jurisdictions. Since tax on the income of foreign subsidiaries (except for certain passive income) is deferred until repatriated, this income can avoid current U.S. taxes and perhaps do so indefinitely. The taxation of passive income (called Subpart F income) has been reduced, perhaps significantly, through the use of "hybrid entities" that are treated differently in different jurisdictions. The use of hybrid entities was greatly expanded by a new regulation (termed "check-the-box") introduced in the late 1990s that had unintended consequences for foreign firms. In addition, earnings from income that is taxed can often be shielded by foreign tax credits on other income. On average very little tax is paid on the foreign source income of U.S. firms. Ample evidence of a significant amount of profit shifting exists, but the revenue cost estimates vary from about $10 billion to $60 billion per year.

Individuals can evade taxes on passive income, such as interest, dividends, and capital gains, by not reporting income earned abroad. In addition, since interest paid to foreign recipients is not taxed, individuals can also evade taxes on U.S. source income by setting up shell corporations and trusts in foreign haven countries to channel funds. There is no general third party reporting of income as is the case for ordinary passive income earned domestically; the IRS relies on qualified intermediaries (QIs) who certify nationality without revealing the beneficial owners. Estimates of the cost of individual evasion have ranged from $40 billion to $70 billion.

Most provisions to address profit shifting by multinational firms would involve changing the tax law: repealing or limiting deferral, limiting the ability of the foreign tax credit to offset income, addressing check-the-box, or even formula apportionment. President Obama's proposals include a proposal to disallow overall deductions and foreign tax credits for deferred income and restrictions on the use of hybrid entities. Provisions to address individual evasion include increased information reporting and provisions to increase enforcement, such as shifting the burden of proof to the taxpayer, increased penalties, and increased resources. Individual tax evasion is the main target of the HIRE Act, the proposed Stop Tax Haven Abuse Act, and the Senate Finance Committee proposals; some revisions are also included in President Obama's plan.

Contents

Tables

Contacts

Introduction

The federal government loses both individual and corporate income tax revenue from the shifting of profits and income into low-tax countries. The revenue losses from this tax avoidance and evasion are difficult to estimate, but some have suggested that the annual cost of offshore tax abuses may be around $100 billion per year.[1] International tax avoidance can arise from wealthy individual investors and from large multinational corporations; it can reflect both legal and illegal actions.

Tax avoidance is sometimes used to refer to a legal reduction in taxes, whereas evasion refers to tax reductions that are illegal. Both types are discussed in this report, although the dividing line is not entirely clear. A multinational firm that constructs a factory in a low-tax jurisdiction rather than in the United States to take advantage of low foreign corporate tax rates is engaged in avoidance, whereas a U.S. citizen who sets up a secret bank account in the Caribbean and does not report the interest income is engaged in evasion. There are, however, many activities, particularly by corporations, that are often referred to as avoidance but could be classified as evasion. One example is transfer pricing, where firms charge low prices for sales to low-tax affiliates but pay high prices for purchases from them. If these prices, which are supposed to be at arms-length, are set at an artificial level, then this activity might be viewed by some as evasion, even if such pricing is not overturned in court because evidence to establish pricing is not available.

Most of the international tax reduction of individuals reflects evasion, and this amount has been estimated to range from about $40 billion to about $70 billion a year.[2] This evasion occurs in part because the United States does not withhold tax on many types of passive income (such as interest) paid to foreign entities; if U.S. individuals can channel their investments through a foreign entity and do not report the holdings of these assets on their tax returns, they evade a tax that they are legally required to pay. In addition, individuals investing in foreign assets may not report income from them.

Corporate tax reductions arising from profit shifting have also been estimated. As discussed below, estimates of the revenue losses from corporate profit shifting vary substantially, ranging from about $10 billion to about $90 billion.

In addition to differentiating between individual and corporate activities, and evasion and avoidance, there are also variations in the features used to characterize tax havens. Some restrictive definitions would limit tax havens to those countries that, in addition to having low or non-existent tax rates on some types of income, also have such other characteristics as the lack of transparency, bank secrecy and the lack of information sharing, and requiring little or no economic activity for an entity to obtain legal status. A definition incorporating compounding factors such as these was used by the Organization for Economic Development and Cooperation (OECD) in their tax shelter initiative. Others, particularly economists, might characterize as a tax haven any low-tax country with a goal of attracting capital, or simply any country that has low or

---

[1] See U.S. Senate Subcommittee on Investigations, *Staff Report on Dividend Tax Abuse*, September 11, 2008.

[2] Joseph Guttentag and Reuven Avi-Yonah, "Closing the International Tax Gap, In Max B. Sawicky, ed. *Bridging the Tax Gap: Addressing the Crisis in Federal Tax Administration*, Washington, DC, Economic Policy Institute, 2005.

non-existent taxes. This report addresses tax havens in their broader sense as well as in their narrower sense.

Although international tax avoidance can be differentiated by whether it is associated with individuals or corporations, whether it is illegal evasion or legal avoidance, and whether it arises in a tax haven narrowly defined or broadly defined, it can also be characterized by what measures might be taken to reduce this loss. In general, revenue losses from individual taxes are more likely to be associated with evasion and more likely to be associated with narrowly defined tax havens, while corporate tax avoidance occurs in both narrowly and broadly defined tax havens and can arise from either legal avoidance or illegal evasion. Evasion is often a problem of lack of information, and remedies may include resources for enforcement, along with incentives and sanctions designed to increase information sharing, and possibly a move towards greater withholding. Avoidance may be more likely to be remedied with changes in the tax code.

Several legislative proposals have been advanced that address international tax issues. President Obama has proposed several international corporate tax revisions which relate to multinational corporations, including profit shifting, as well as individual tax evasion. Some of the provisions relating to multinationals had earlier been included in a bill introduced in the 110th Congress by Chairman Rangel of the Ways and Means Committee (H.R. 3970). Major revisions to corporate international tax rules are also included in S. 3018, a general tax reform act introduced by Senators Wyden and Gregg in the 111th Congress, and a similar bill, S. 727, introduced by Senators Wyden and Coats in the 112th Congress.[3] This bill has provisions to tax foreign source income currently, which could limit the benefits from corporate profit shifting. Ways and Means Chairman Dave Camp has proposed a lower corporate rate combined with a move to a territorial tax system (which would exempt foreign source income). Because a territorial tax could increase the scope for profit shifting, the proposal contains detailed provisions to address these issues. A territorial tax proposal has also been introduced by Senator Enzi (S. 2091).[4]

The Senate Permanent Subcommittee on Investigations has been engaged in international tax investigations since 2001, holding hearings proposing legislation.[5] In the 111th Congress, the Stop Tax Haven Abuse Act, S. 506, was introduced by the chairman of that committee, Senator Levin, with a companion bill, H.R. 1265, introduced by Representative Doggett. The Senate Finance Committee also has circulated draft proposals addressing individual tax evasion issues. A number of these anti-evasion provisions (including provisions in President Obama's budget outline) have been adopted in the Hiring Incentives to Restore Employment (HIRE) Act, P.L. 111-147. In the 112th Congress, a revised version of the Stop Tax Haven Abuse Act (H.R. 2669 and S. 1346) was introduced. On the 111th Congress, S. 386, introduced by Chairman Leahy of the Senate Judiciary Committee, would have expanded the money-laundering provisions to include tax evasion and provide additional funding for the tax division of the Justice Department. These tax-related provisions were not included in the final law, P.L. 111-21. S. 569, also introduced by Chairman Levin, would impose requirements on the states for determination of beneficial owners of

---

[3] See "Obama Backs Corporate Tax Cut If Won't Raise Deficit," *Bloomberg*, January 25, 2011, http://www.bloomberg.com/news/2011-01-26/obama-backs-cut-in-u-s-corporate-tax-rate-only-if-it-won-t-affect-deficit.html.

[4] See CRS Report R42624, *Moving to a Territorial Income Tax: Options and Challenges*, by Jane G. Gravelle, for a discussion of the Camp and Enzi proposals.

[5] For a chronology, see Martin Sullivan, "Proposals to Fight Offshore Tax Evasion, Part 3," *Tax Notes* May 4, 2009, p. 517.

---

corporations formed under their laws. This proposal has implications for the potential use of incorporation in certain states as a part of an international tax haven plan.

The Permanent Subcommittee also released a study of profit-shifting by multinationals in preparation for a hearing on September 20, 2012.[6]

The first section of this report reviews what countries might be considered tax havens, including a discussion of the Organization for Economic Development and Cooperation (OECD) initiatives and lists. The next two sections discuss, in turn, the corporate profit-shifting mechanisms and evidence on the existence and magnitude of profit shifting activity. The following two sections provide the same analysis for individual tax evasion. The report concludes with overviews of alternative policy options and a summary of specific legislative proposals.

Where Are the Tax Havens?

There is no precise definition of a tax haven. The OECD initially defined the following features of tax havens: no or low taxes, lack of effective exchange of information, lack of transparency, and no requirement of substantial activity.[7] Other lists have been developed in legislative proposals and by researchers. Also, a number of other jurisdictions have been identified as having tax haven characteristics.

Formal Lists of Tax Havens

The OECD created an initial list of tax havens in 2000. A similar list was used in S. 396, introduced in the 110th Congress, which would treat firms incorporated in certain tax havens as domestic companies; the only difference between this list and the OECD list was the exclusion of the U.S. Virgin Islands from the list in S. 396. Legislation introduced in the 111th Congress to address tax haven abuse (S. 506, H.R. 1265) uses a different list taken from IRS court filings, but has many countries in common. The definition by the OECD excluded low-tax jurisdictions, some of which are OECD members, that were thought by many to be tax havens, such as Ireland and Switzerland. These countries were included in an important study of tax havens by Hines and Rice.[8] GAO also provided a list.[9]

Table 1 lists the countries that appear on various lists, arranged by geographic location. These tax havens tend to be concentrated in certain areas, including the Caribbean and West Indies and Europe, locations close to large developed countries. There are 50 altogether.

---

[6] Memo on Offshore Profit Shifting and the U.S. Tax Code, at http://www.levin.senate.gov/newsroom/press/release/subcommittee-hearing-to-examine-billions-of-dollars-in-us-tax-avoidance-by-multinational-corporations/?section=alltypes.

[7] Organization for Economic Development and Cooperation, *Harmful Tax Competition: An Emerging Global Issue*, 1998, p. 23.

[8] J.R. Hines and E.M. Rice, "Fiscal Paradise: Foreign Tax havens and American Business," *Quarterly Journal of Economics*, vol. 109, February 1994, pp. 149-182.

[9] Government Accountability Office, International Taxation: Large U.S. Corporations and Federal Contractors with Subsidiaries in Jurisdictions Listed as Tax Havens or Financial Privacy Jurisdictions, GAO-op-157, December 2008.

Table 1. Countries Listed on Various Tax Haven Lists

Caribbean/West Indies	Anguilla, Antigua and Barbuda, Aruba, Bahamas, Barbados,[d,e] British Virgin Islands, Cayman Islands, Dominica, Grenada, Montserrat,[a] Netherlands Antilles, St. Kitts and Nevis, St. Lucia, St. Vincent and Grenadines, Turks and Caicos, U.S. Virgin Islands[a,e]
Central America	Belize, Costa Rica,[b,c] Panama
Coast of East Asia	Hong Kong,[b,e] Macau,[a,b,e] Singapore[b]
Europe/Mediterranean	Andorra,[a] Channel Islands (Guernsey and Jersey),[e] Cyprus,[e] Gibralter, Isle of Man,[e] Ireland,[a,b,e] Liechtenstein, Luxembourg,[a,b,e] Malta,[e] Monaco,[a] San Marino,[a,e] Switzerland[a,b]
Indian Ocean	Maldives,[a,d] Mauritius,[a,c,e] Seychelles[a,e]
Middle East	Bahrain, Jordan,[a,b] Lebanon[a,b]
North Atlantic	Bermuda[e]
Pacific, South Pacific	Cook Islands, Marshall Islands,[a] Samoa, Nauru,[c] Niue,[a,c] Tonga,[a,c,d] Vanuatu
West Africa	Liberia

Sources: Organization for Economic Development and Cooperation (OECD), *Towards Global Tax Competition*, 2000; Dhammika Dharmapala and James R. Hines, "Which Countries Become Tax Havens?" Journal of Public Economics, Vol. 93, October 2009, pp. 1058-1068; Tax Justice Network, "Identifying Tax Havens and Offshore Finance Centers: http://www.taxjustice.net/cms/upload/pdf/Identifying_Tax_Havens_Jul_07.pdf. The OECD's "gray" list is posted at http://www.oecd.org/dataoecd/38/14/42497950.pdf. The countries in Table 1 are the same as the countries, with the exception of Tonga, in a recent GAO Report, *International Taxation: Large U.S. Corporations and Federal Contractors with Subsidiaries in Jurisdictions Listed as Tax Havens or Financial Privacy Jurisdictions*, GAO-09-157, December 2008.

Notes: The Dharmapala and HInes paper cited above reproduces the Hines and Rice list. That list was more oriented to business issues; four countries—Ireland, Jordan, Luxembourg, and Switzerland—appear only on that list. The Hines and Rice list is older and is itself based on earlier lists; some countries on those earlier lists were eliminated because they had higher tax rates.

St. Kitts may also be referred to as St. Christopher. The Channel Islands are sometimes listed as a group and sometimes Jersey and Guernsey are listed separately. S. 506 and H.R. 1245 specifically mention Jersey, and also refer to Gurensey/Sark/Alderney; the latter two are islands associated with Guernsey.

a.   Not included in S. 506, H.R. 1245.

b.   Not included in original OECD tax haven list.

c.   Not included in Hines and Rice (1994).

d.   Removed from OECD's List; Subsequently determined they should not be included.

e.   Not included in OECD's "gray" list as of August 17, 2009; currently on the OECD "white" list. Note that the "gray" list is divided into countries that are tax havens and countries that are other financial centers. The latter classification includes three countries listed in Table 1 (Luxembourg, Singapore, and Switzerland) and five that are not (Austria, Belgium, Brunei, Chile, and Guatemala). Of the four countries moved from the "black" to the "gray" list, one, Costa Rica, is in **Table 1** and three, Malaysia, Uruguay, and the Philippines, are not.

Developments in the OECD Tax Haven List

The OECD list, the most prominent list, has changed over time. Nine of the countries in **Table 1** did not appear on the earliest OECD list. These countries not appearing on the original list tend to be more developed larger countries and include some that are members of the OECD (e.g., Switzerland and Luxembourg).

It is also important to distinguish between OECD's original list and its blacklist. OECD subsequently focused on information exchange and removed countries from a "blacklist if they agree to cooperate." OECD initially examined 47 jurisdictions and identified a number as not meeting the criteria for a tax haven; it also initially excluded six countries with advance agreements to share information (Bermuda, the Cayman Islands, Cyprus, Malta, Mauritius, and San Marino). The 2000 OECD blacklist included 35 countries; this list did not include the six countries eliminated due to advance agreement. The OECD had also subsequently determined that three countries should not be included in the list of tax havens (Barbados, the Maldives, and Tonga). Over time, as more tax havens made agreements to share information, the blacklist dwindled until it included only three countries: Andorra, Liechtenstein, and Monaco.

A study of the OECD initiative on global tax coordination by Sharman, also discussed in a book review by Sullivan, argues that the reduction in the OECD list was not because of actual progress towards cooperation so much as due to the withdrawal of U.S. support in 2001, which resulted in the OECD focusing on information on request and not requiring reforms until all parties had signed on.[10] This analysis suggests that the large countries were not successful in this initiative to rein in on tax havens. A similar analysis by Spencer and Sharman suggests little real progress has been made in reducing tax haven practices.[11]

Interest in tax haven actions has increased recently. The scandals surrounding the Swiss bank UBS AG (UBS) and the Liechtenstein Global Trust Group (LGT), which led to legal actions by the United States and other countries, focused greater attention on international tax issues, primarily information reporting and individual evasion.[12] The credit crunch and provision of public funds to banks has also heightened public interest. The tax haven issue was revived recently with a meeting of the G20 industrialized and developing countries that proposed sanctions, and a number of countries began to indicate commitments to information sharing agreements.[13]

The OECD currently has three lists: a "white list" of countries implementing an agreed-upon standard, a "gray" list of countries that have committed to such a standard, and a "black" list of countries that have not committed. On April 7, 2009, the last four countries on the "black" list, which were countries not included on the original OECD list—Costa Rica, Malaysia, the Philippines, and Uruguay—were moved to the "gray" list.[14] The gray list includes countries not identified as tax havens but as "other financial centers." According to news reports, Hong Kong and Macau were omitted from the OECD's list because of objections from China, but are mentioned in a footnote as having committed to the standards; they also noted that a "recent flurry of commitments brought 11 jurisdictions, including Austria, Liechtenstein, Luxembourg,

---

[10] J. C. Sharman, *Havens in a Storm, The Struggle for Global Tax Regulation*, Cornell University Press, Ithaca, New York, 2006; Martin A. Sullivan, "Lessons From the Last War on Tax Havens," *Tax Notes*, July 30, 2007, pp. 327-337.

[11] David Spencer and J.C. Sharman, International Tax Cooperation, *Journal of International Taxation*, published in three parts in December 2007, pp. 35-49, January 2008, pp. 27-44, 64, February 2008, pp. 39-58.

[12] For a discussion of these cases see Joint Committee on Taxation *Tax Compliance and Enforcement Issues With Respect to Offshore Entities and Accounts*, JCX-23-09, March 30, 2009. The discussion of UBS begins on p. 31 and the discussion of LGT begins on p. 40. This document also discusses the inquiries of the Permanent Subcommittee on Investigations of the Senate Homeland Security Committee relating to these cases.

[13] Anthony Faiola and Mary Jordan, "Tax-Haven Blacklist Stirs Nations: After G-20 Issues mandate, Many Rush to Get Off Roll," *Washington Post*, April 4, p. A7.

[14] This announcement by the OECD was posted at http://www.oecd.org/document/0/ 0,3343,en_2649_34487_42521280_1_1_1_1,00.html.

Singapore, and Switzerland into the committed category."[15] As of May 18, 2012, only one country (Nauru) appeared on the gray list for tax havens and one (Guatemala) appeared on the gray list for financial centers.[16]

Many countries that were listed on the OECD's original blacklist protested because of the negative publicity and many now point to having signed agreements to negotiate tax information exchange agreements (TIEA) and some have negotiated agreements. The identification of tax havens can have legal ramifications if laws and sanctions are contingent on that identification, as is the case of some current proposals in the United States and of potential sanctions by international bodies.

Other Jurisdictions With Tax Haven Characteristics

Criticisms have been made by a range of commentators that many countries are tax havens or have aspects of tax havens and have been overlooked. These jurisdictions include major countries such as the United States, the UK, the Netherlands, Denmark, Hungary, Iceland, Israel, Portugal, and Canada. Attention has also been directed at three states in the United States: Delaware, Nevada, and Wyoming. Finally, there are a number of smaller countries or areas in countries, such as Campione d'Italia, an Italian town located within Switzerland, that have been characterized as tax havens.

A country not on the list in **Table 1**, but which is often considered a tax haven, especially for corporations, is the Netherlands, which allows firms to reduce taxes on dividends and capital gains from subsidiaries and has a wide range of treaties that reduce taxes.[17] In 2006, for example, Bono and other members of the U2 band moved their music publishing company from Ireland to the Netherlands after Ireland changed its tax treatment of music royalties.[18] A recent newspaper report explained the role of the Netherlands in facilitating movement to tax havens through provisions such as the various "Dutch sandwiches," that allow money to be funneled out of other countries that would charge withholding taxes to non-European countries, to be passed on in turn to tax havens such as Bermuda and the Cayman Islands.[19]

Some have identified the United States and the United Kingdom as having tax haven characteristics. Luxembourg Prime Minister Jean-Claude Junker urged other EU member states to challenge the United States for tax havens in Delaware, Nevada, and Wyoming.[20] One website offering offshore services mentions, in their view, several overlooked tax havens which include

---

[15] David D. Stewart, "G-20 Declares End to Bank Secrecy as OECD Issues Tiered List," *Tax Notes*, April 6, 2009, pp. 38-39.

[16] Organization for Economic Development and Cooperation, http://www.oecd.org/dataoecd/50/0/43606256.pdf.

[17] See, for example, Micheil van Dijk, Francix Weyzig, and Richard Murphy, *The Netherlands: A Tax Haven?* SOMO (Centre for Research on Multinational Corporations), Amersterdam, 2007 and Rosanne Altshuler and Harry Grubert, "Governments and Multinational Corporations in the Race to the Bottom, Tax Notes, February 27, 2009, pp. 979-992.

[18] Fergal O'Brien, "Bono, Preacher on Poverty, Tarnishes Halo Irish Tax Move," October 15, 2006, Bloomberg.com, http://bloomberg.com/apps/news?pid=20601109&refer=home&sid=aef6sR60oDgM#.

[19] See Jesse Drucker, "Google 2.4% Rate Shows How $60 Billion Lost to Tax Loopholes," *Bloomberg*, October 21, 2010, posted at http://www.bloomberg.com/news/2010-10-21/google-2-4-rate-shows-how-60-billion-u-s-revenue-lost-to-tax-loopholes.html and "Yahoo, Dell Swell Netherlands' $13 Trillion Tax Haven," *Bloomberg*, January 23, 2013, posted at http://www.bloomberg.com/news/2013-01-23/yahoo-dell-swell-netherlands-13-trillion-tax-haven.html.

[20] Charles Gnaedinger, "Luxembourg P.M Calls out U.S. States as Tax Havens" *Tax Notes International*, April 6, 2009, p. 13.

the United States, United Kingdom, Denmark, Iceland, Israel, and Portugal's Madeira Island.[21] (Others on their list and not listed in **Table 1** were Hungary, Brunei, Uruguay, and Labuan [Malaysia]).[22] In the case of the United States the article mentions the lack of reporting requirements and the failure to tax interest and other exempt passive income paid to foreign entities, the limited liability corporation which allows a flexible corporate vehicle not subject to taxation, and the ease of incorporating in certain states (Delaware, Nevada, and Wyoming).

Another website includes in its list of tax havens Delaware, Wyoming, and Puerto Rico, along with other jurisdictions not listed in **Table 1**: the Netherlands, Campione d'Italia, a separate listing for Sark (identified as the only remaining "fiscal paradise"), the United Kingdom, and a coming discussion for Canada.[23] Sark is an island country associated with Guernsey, part of the Channel Islands, and Campione d'Italia is an Italian town located within Switzerland.

The Economist reported a study by a political scientist experimenting with setting up sham corporations; the author succeeded in incorporating in Wyoming and Nevada, as well as the United Kingdom and several other places.[24] Michael McIntyre discusses three U.S. practices that aid international evasion: the failure to collect information on tax exempt interest income paid to foreign entities, the system of foreign institutions that act as qualified intermediaries (see discussion below) but do not reveal their clients, and the practices of states such as Delaware and Wyoming that allow people to keep secret their identities as stockholder or depositor.[25]

In a meeting in late April 2009, Eduardo Silva, of the Cayman Islands Financial Services Association, claimed that Delaware, Nevada, Wyoming, and the United Kingdom were the greatest offenders with respect to, among other issues, tax fraud. He suggested that Nevada and Wyoming were worse than Delaware because they permit companies to have bearer shares, which allows anonymous ownership. A U.S. participant at the conference noted that legislation in the United States, S. 569, would require disclosure of beneficial owners in the United States.[26]

In addition, any country with a low tax rate could be considered as a potential location for shifting income to. In addition to Ireland, three other countries in the OECD not included in **Table 1** have tax rates below 20%: Iceland, Poland, and the Slovak Republic.[27] Most of the eastern European countries not included in the OECD have tax rates below 20%.[28]

The Tax Justice Network probably has the largest list of tax havens, and includes some specific cities and areas.[29] In addition to the countries listed in **Table 1**, they include in the Americas and Caribbean, New York and Uruguay; in Africa, Mellila, Sao Tome e Principe, Somalia, and South Africa; in the Middle East and Asia, Dubai, Labuan (Malaysia), Tel Aviv, and Taipei; in Europe,

---

[21] http://www.offshore-fox.com/offshore-corporations/offshore_corporations_0401.html.

[22] Another offshore website lists in addition to the countries in Table 1 Austria, Campione d'Italia, Denmark, Hungary, Iceland, Madeira, Russian Federation, United Kingdom, Brunei, Dubai, Lebanon, Canada, Puerto Rico, South Africa, New Zealand, Labuan, Uruguay, and the United States. See http://www.mydeltaquest.com/english/.

[23] http://www.offshore-manual.com/taxhavens/.

[24] "Haven Hypocrisy," *The Economist*, March 26, 2008.

[25] Michael McIntyre, "A Program for International Tax Reform," *Tax Notes*, February 23, 2009, pp. 1021-1026.

[26] Charles Gnaedinger, "U.S.,Cayman Islands Debate Tax Haven Status," *Tax Notes*, May 4, 2009, p. 548-545.

[27] http://www.oecd.org/document/60/0,3343,en_2649_34897_1942460_1_1_1_1,00.html.

[28] For tax rates see http://www.worldwide-tax.com/index.asp#partthree.

[29] Tax Justice Network, *Tax Us if You Can*, September, 2005.

Alderney, Belgium, Campione d'Italia, City of London, Dublin, Ingushetia, Madeira, Sark, Trieste, Turkish Republic of Northern Cyprus, and Frankfurt; and in the Indian and Pacific oceans, the Marianas. The only county listed in **Table 1** and not included in their list was Jordan.

Methods of Corporate Tax Avoidance

U.S. multinationals are not taxed on income earned by foreign subsidiaries until it is repatriated to the U.S. parent as dividends, although some passive and related company income that is easily shifted is taxed currently under anti-abuse rules referred to as Subpart F. (Foreign affiliates or subsidiaries that are majority owned U.S. owned are referred to as controlled foreign corporations, or CFCs, and many of these related firms are wholly owned.) Taxes on income that is repatriated (or, less commonly, earned by branches and taxed currently) are allowed a credit for foreign income taxes paid. (A part of a parent company treated as a branch is not a separate entity for tax purposes, and all income is part of the parent's income.)

Foreign tax credits are limited to the amount of tax imposed by the United States, so that they, in theory, cannot offset taxes on domestic income. This limit is imposed on an overall basis, allowing excess credits in high-tax countries to offset U.S. tax liability on income earned in low-tax countries, although separate limits apply to passive and active income. Other countries either employ this system of deferral and credit or, more commonly, exempt income earned in foreign jurisdictions. Most countries have some form of anti-abuse rules similar to Subpart F.

If a firm can shift profits to a low-tax jurisdiction from a high-tax one, its taxes will be reduced without affecting other aspects of the company. Tax differences also affect real economic activity, which in turn affects revenues, but it is this artificial shifting of profits that is the focus of this report.[30]

Because the United States taxes all income earned in its borders as well as imposing a residual tax on income earned abroad by U.S. persons, tax avoidance relates both to U.S. parent companies shifting profits abroad to low-tax jurisdictions and the shifting of profits out of the United States by foreign parents of U.S. subsidiaries. In the case of U.S. multinationals, one study suggested that about half the difference between profitability in low-tax and high-tax countries, which could arise from artificial income shifting, was due to transfers of intellectual property (or intangibles) and most of the rest through the allocation of debt.[31] However, a study examining import and export prices suggests a very large effect of transfer pricing in goods (as discussed below).[32] Some evidence of the importance of intellectual property can also be found from the types of firms that repatriated profits abroad following a temporary tax reduction enacted in 2004; one-third of the repatriations were in the pharmaceutical and medicine industry and almost 20% in the computer and electronic equipment industry.[33]

---

[30] Effects on economic activity are addressed in CRS Report RL34115, *Reform of U.S. International Taxation: Alternatives*, by Jane G. Gravelle.

[31] Harry Grubert, "Intangible Income, Intercompany Transactions, Income Shifting and the Choice of Locations," *National Tax Journal*, vol. 56, March 2003, Part II, pp. 221-242.

[32] Simon J. Pak and John S. Zdanowicz, *U.S. Trade With the World, An Estimate of 2001 Lost U.S. Federal Income Tax Revenues Due to Over-Invoiced Imports and Under-Invoiced Exports*, October 31, 2002.

[33] CRS Report R40178, *Tax Cuts on Repatriation Earnings as Economic Stimulus: An Economic Analysis*, by Donald J. Marples and Jane G. Gravelle.

Allocation of Debt and Earnings Stripping

One method of shifting profits from a high-tax jurisdiction to a low-tax one is to borrow more in the high-tax jurisdiction and less in the low-tax one. This shifting of debt can be achieved without changing the overall debt exposure of the firm. A more specific practice is referred to as earnings stripping, where either debt is associated with related firms or unrelated debt is not subject to tax by the recipient. As an example of the former earnings stripping method, a foreign parent may lend to its U.S. subsidiary. Alternatively, an unrelated foreign borrower not subject to tax on U.S. interest income might lend to a U.S. firm.

The U.S. tax code currently contains provisions to address interest deductions and earnings stripping. It applies an allocation of the U.S. parent's interest for purposes of the limit on the foreign tax credit. The amount of foreign source income is reduced when part of U.S. interest is allocated and the maximum amount of foreign tax credits taken is limited, a provision that affects firms with excess foreign tax credits.[34] There is no allocation rule, however, to address deferral, so that a U.S. parent could operate its subsidiary with all equity finance in a low-tax jurisdiction and take all of the interest on the overall firm's debt as a deduction. A bill introduced in 2007 (H.R. 3970) by Chairman Rangel of the Ways and Means Committee would introduce such an allocation rule, so that a portion of interest and other overhead costs would not be deducted until the income is repatriated.[35] This provision is also included in President Obama's proposals for international tax revision.

While allocation-of-interest approaches could be used to address allocation of interest to high-tax countries in the case of U.S. multinationals, they cannot be applied to U.S. subsidiaries of foreign corporations. To limit the scope of earnings stripping in either case, the United States has thin capitalization rules. (Most of the United States' major trading partners have similar rules.) A section of the Internal Revenue Code (163(j)) applies to a corporation with a debt-to-equity ratio above 1.5 to 1 and with net interest exceeding 50% of adjusted taxable income (generally taxable income plus interest plus depreciation). Interest in excess of the 50% limit paid to a related corporation is not deductible if the corporation is not subject to U.S. income tax. This interest restriction also applies to interest paid to unrelated parties that are not taxed to the recipient.

The possibility of earnings stripping received more attention after a number of U.S. firms inverted, that is, arranged to move their parent firm abroad so that U.S. operations became a subsidiary of that parent. The American Jobs Creation Act (AJCA) of 2004 addressed the general problem of inversion by treating firms that subsequently inverted as U.S. firms. During consideration of this legislation there were also proposals for broader earnings stripping restrictions as an approach to this problem that would have reduced the excess interest deductions. This general earnings stripping proposal was not adopted. However, the AJCA mandated a Treasury Department study on this and other issues; that study focused on U.S. subsidiaries of foreign parents and was not able to find clear evidence on the magnitude.[36]

---

[34] In 2004 the interest allocation rules were changed to allocate worldwide interest, but the implementation of that provision was delayed and has not yet taken place. See CRS Report RL34494, *The Foreign Tax Credit's Interest Allocation Rules*, by Jane G. Gravelle and Donald J. Marples.

[35] See CRS Report RL34249, *The Tax Reduction and Reform Act of 2007: An Overview*, by Jane G. Gravelle.

[36] U.S. Department of Treasury, *Report to Congress on Earnings Stripping, Transfer Pricing and U.S. Income Tax Treaties*, November 2007.

An noted in the Treasury's mandated study, there is relatively straightforward evidence that U.S. multinationals allocate more interest to high-tax jurisdictions, but it is more difficult to assess earnings stripping by foreign parents of U.S. subsidiaries, because the entire firm's accounts are not available. The Treasury study focused on this issue and used an approach that had been used in the past of comparing these subsidiaries to U.S. firms. The study was not able to provide conclusive evidence about the shifting of profits out of the United States due to high leverage rates for U.S. subsidiaries of foreign firms but did find evidence of shifting for inverted firms.

Transfer Pricing

The second major way that firms can shift profits from high-tax to low-tax jurisdictions is through the pricing of goods and services sold between affiliates. To properly reflect income, prices of goods and services sold by related companies should be the same as the prices that would be paid by unrelated parties. By lowering the price of goods and services sold by parents and affiliates in high-tax jurisdictions and raising the price of purchases, income can be shifted.

An important and growing issue of transfer pricing is with the transfers to rights to intellectual property, or intangibles. If a patent developed in the United States is licensed to an affiliate in a low-tax country income will be shifted if the royalty or other payment is lower than the true value of the license. For many goods there are similar products sold or other methods (such as cost plus a markup) that can be used to determine whether prices are set appropriately. Intangibles, such as new inventions or new drugs, tend not to have comparables, and it is very difficult to know the royalty that would be paid in an arms-length price. Therefore, intangibles represent particular problems for policing transfer pricing.

Investment in intangibles is favorably treated in the United States because costs, other than capital equipment and buildings, are expensed for research and development, which is also eligible for a tax credit. In addition, advertising to establish brand names is also deductible. Overall these treatments tend to produce an effective low, zero, or negative tax rate for overall investment in intangibles. Thus, there are significant incentives to make these investments in the United States. On average, the benefit of tax deductions or credits when making the investment tend to offset the future taxes on the return to the investment. However, for those investments that tend to be successful, it is advantageous to shift profits to a low-tax jurisdiction, so that there are tax savings on investment and little or no tax on returns. As a result, these investments can be subject to negative tax rates, or subsidies, which can be significant.

Transfer pricing rules with respect to intellectual property are further complicated because of cost sharing agreements, where different affiliates contribute to the cost.[37] If an intangible is already partially developed by the parent firm, affiliates contribute a buy-in payment. It is very difficult to determine arms-length pricing in these cases where a technology is partially developed and there is risk associated with the expected outcome. One study found some evidence that firms with cost sharing arrangements were more likely to engage in profit shifting.[38]

---

[37] The Treasury Department recently issued new proposed regulations relating to cost sharing arrangements. See Treasury Decision 9441, Federal Register, vol. 74, No. 2, January 5, 2009, pp. 340-391. These rules include a periodic adjustment which would, among other aspects, examine outcomes. See "Cost Sharing Periodic Payments Not Automatic, Officials Say," *Tax Notes*, February 23, 2009, p. 955.

[38] Michael McDonald, "Income Shifting from Transfer Pricing: Further Evidence from Tax Return Data," U.S. Department of the Treasury, Office of Tax Analysis, OTA Technical Working Paper 2, July 2008.

One problem with shifting profits to some tax haven jurisdictions is that, if real activity is necessary to produce the intangible these countries may not have labor and other resources to undertake the activity. However, firms have developed techniques to take advantage of tax laws in other countries to achieve both a productive operation while shifting profits to no-tax jurisdictions. An example is the "double Irish, Dutch sandwich" method that has been used by some U.S. firms, which, as exposed in news articles, has been used by Google.[39] In this arrangement, the U.S. firm transfers its intangible asset to an Irish holding company. This company has a subsidiary sales company that sells advertising (the source of Google's revenues) to Europe. However, sandwiched between the Irish holding company and the Irish sales subsidiary is a Dutch subsidiary, which collects royalties from the sales subsidiary and transfer them to the Irish holding company. The Irish holding company claims company management (and tax home) in Bermuda, with a 0% tax rate, for purposes of the corporate income tax. This scheme allows the Irish operation to avoid the even the lower Irish tax of 12.5%, and also, by using the Dutch sandwich, to avoid Irish withholding taxes (which are not due on payments to European Union companies). More recently, European countries have complained about companies such as Google, Apple, Amazon, Facebook and Starbucks in some cases using this scheme. Profits can also be shifted directly to a tax haven as in the case of Yahoo, where the Dutch intermediary can transfer profits directly to the tax haven (in this case, the Cayman islands) because it does not collect a withholding tax as would be the case with France or Ireland.[40]

Contract Manufacturing

When a subsidiary is set up in a low-tax country and profit shifting occurs, as in the acquisition of rights to an intangible, a further problem occurs: this low-tax country may not be a desirable place to actually manufacture and sell the product. For example, an Irish subsidiary's market may be in Germany and it would be desirable to manufacture in Germany. But to earn profits in Germany with its higher tax rate does not minimize taxes. Instead the Irish firm may contract with a German firm as a contract manufacturer, who will produce the item for cost plus a fixed markup. Subpart F taxes on a current basis certain profits from sales income, so the arrangement must be structured to qualify as an exception from this rule. There are complex and changing regulations on this issue.[41]

Check-the-Box, Hybrid Entities, and Hybrid Instruments

Another technique for shifting profit to low-tax jurisdictions was greatly expanded with the "check-the-box" provisions. These provisions were originally intended to simplify questions of whether a firm was a corporation or partnership. Their application to foreign circumstances

[39] Jesse Drucker, "Google 2.4% Rate Shows How $60 Billion Lost to Tax Loopholes," *Bloomberg*, October 21, 2010, posted at http://www.bloomberg.com/news/2010-10-21/google-2-4-rate-shows-how-60-billion-u-s-revenue-lost-to-tax-loopholes.html, and "Yahoo, Dell Swell Netherlands' $13 Trillion Tax Haven," *Bloomberg*, January 23, 2013, posted at http://www.bloomberg.com/news/2013-01-23/yahoo-dell-swell-netherlands-13-trillion-tax-haven.html.

[40]Szu Ping Chang, "Facebook Hid £440m in Cayman Islands Tax Haven," The Telegraph, December 23, 2012, at http://www.telegraph.co.uk/finance/newsbysector/banksandfinance/9763615/Facebook-hid-440m-in-Cayman-Islands-tax-haven.html; Lori Hinnant, "Europe Takes On Tech Giants And Tax Havens," *Associated Press*, at http://www.manufacturing.net/news/2012/12/europe-takes-on-tech-giants-and-tax-havens.

[41] See for example William W. Chip, "'Manufacturing' Foreign Base Company Sales Income," *Tax Notes*, November 19, 2007, p. 803-808.

through the "disregarded entity" rules has led to the expansion of hybrid entities, where an entity can be recognized as a corporation by one jurisdiction but not by another. For example, a U.S. parent's subsidiary in a low-tax country can lend to its subsidiary in a high-tax country, with the interest deductible because the high-tax country recognizes the firm as a separate corporation. Normally, interest received by the subsidiary in the low-tax country would be considered passive or "tainted" income subject to current U.S. tax under Subpart F. However, under check-the-box rules, the high-tax corporation can elect to be disregarded as a separate entity, and thus from the perspective of the United States there is no interest income paid because the two are the same entity. Check-the-box and similar hybrid entity operations can also be used to avoid other types of Subpart F income, for example from contract manufacturing arrangements. According to Sicular, this provision, which began as a regulation, has been effectively codified, albeit temporarily.[42]

Hybrid entities relate to issues other than Subpart F. For example, a reverse hybrid entity can be used to allow U.S. corporations to benefit from the foreign tax credit without having to recognize the underlying income. As an example, a U.S. parent can set up a holding company in a county that is treated as a disregarded entity, and the holding company can own a corporation that is treated as a partnership in another foreign jurisdiction. Under flow through rules, the holding company is liable for the foreign tax and, because it is not a separate entity, the U.S. parent corporation is therefore liable, but the income can be retained in the foreign corporation that is viewed as a separate corporate entity from the U.S. point of view. In this case, the entity is structured so that it is a partnership for foreign purposes but a corporation for U.S. purposes.[43]

In addition to hybrid entities that achieve tax benefits by being treated differently in the United States and the foreign jurisdiction, there are also hybrid instruments that can avoid taxation by being treated as debt in one jurisdiction and equity in another.[44]

Cross Crediting and Sourcing Rules for Foreign Tax Credits

Income from a low-tax country that is received in the United States can escape taxes because of cross crediting: the use of excess foreign taxes paid in one jurisdiction or on one type of income to offset U.S. tax that would be due on other income. In some periods in the past the foreign tax credit limit was proposed on a country-by-country basis, although that rule proved to be difficult to enforce given the potential to use holding companies. Foreign tax credits have subsequently been separated into different baskets to limit cross crediting; these baskets were reduced from nine to two (active and passive) in the American Jobs Creation Act of 2004 (P.L. 108-357).

Because firms can choose when to repatriate income, they can arrange realizations to maximize the benefits of the overall limit on the foreign tax credit. That is, firms that have income from jurisdictions with taxes in excess of U.S. taxes can also elect to realize income from jurisdictions with low taxes and use the excess credits to offset U.S. tax due on that income. Studies suggest

---

[42] See David R. Sicular, "The New Look-Through Rule: W(h)ither Subpart F? *Tax Notes*, April 23, 2007, pp. 349-378 for a discussion of the look-through rules under Section 954(c)(6).

[43] For a discussion of reverse hybrids see Joseph M. Calianno and J. Michael Cornett, "Guardian Revision: Proposed Regulations Attach Guardian and Reverse Hybrids," *Tax Notes International*, October 2006, pp. 305-316.

[44] See Sean Foley, "U.S. Outbound: Cross border Hybrid Instrument Transactions to gain Increased Scrutiny During IRS Audit," http://www.internationaltaxreview.com/?Page=10&PUBID=35&ISS=24101&SID=692834&TYPE=20. Andrei Kraymal, International Hybrid Instruments: Jurisdiction Dependent Characterization, *Houston Business and Tax Law Journal*, 2005, http://www.hbtlj.org/v05/v05Krahmalar.pdf.

that between cross crediting and deferral, U.S. multinationals typically pay virtually no U.S. tax on foreign source income.[45]

This ability to reduce U.S. tax due to cross crediting is increased, it can be argued, because income that should be considered U.S. source income is treated as foreign source income, thereby raising the foreign tax credit limit. This includes income from U.S. exports which is U.S. source income, because a tax provision (referred to as the title passage rule) allows half of export income to be allocated to the country in which the title passes. Another important type of income that is considered foreign source and thus can be shielded with foreign tax credits is royalty income from active business, which has become an increasingly important source of foreign income. This benefit can occur in high-tax countries because royalties are generally deductible from income. (Note that the shifting of income due to transfer pricing of intangibles, advantageous in low-tax countries, is a different issue.) Interest income is another type of income that may benefit from this foreign tax credit rule.

Since all of this income arises from investment in the United States, one could argue that this income is appropriately U.S. source income, or that, failing that, it should be put in a different foreign tax credit basket so that excess credits generated by dividends cannot be used to offset such income. Two studies, by Grubert and by Grubert and Altshuler, have discussed this sourcing rule in the context of a proposal to eliminate the tax on active dividends.[46] In that proposal, the revenue loss from exempting active dividends from U.S. tax would be offset by gains from taxes on royalties.

In addition to these general policy issues, there are numerous other narrower techniques that might be used to enhance foreign tax credits; a number of these are the focus of legislation in H.R. 4213, the American Jobs and Loophole Closing Act.

The Magnitude of Corporate Profit Shifting

This section examines the evidence on the existence and magnitude of profit shifting and the techniques that are most likely to contribute to it.

Evidence on the Scope of Profit Shifting

There is ample, and simple, evidence that profits appear in countries inconsistent with an economic motivation. This section first examines the profit share of income of controlled corporations compared to the share of gross domestic product.[47] The first set of countries, acting

---

[45] Government Accountability Office, U.S. Multinational Corporations: Effective Tax Rates are Correlated With Where Income is Reported, GAO-08-950, August 2008. Melissa Costa and Jennifer Gravelle, "Taxing Multinational Corporations: Average Tax Rates," Tax Law Review, vo. 65, no. 3, spring 2012, pp. 391-414; Jennifer Gravelle, Who Will Benefit from a Territorial Tax, Presented at the 105th Conference of the National Tax Association, 2012.

[46] Harry Grubert, "Tax Credits, Source Rules, Trade and electronic Commerce: Behavioral Margins and the Design of International Tax Systems. *Tax Law Review*, vol. 58, January 2005; also issued as a CESIFO Working Paper no. 1366, December 2004; Harry Grubert and Rosanne Altshuler, "Corporate Taxes in a World Economy: Reforming the Taxation of Cross-Border Income," in John W. Diamond and George Zodrow, eds., *Fundamental Tax Reform: Issues, Choices and Implications*, Cambridge, MIT Press, 2008.

[47] Data on earnings and profits of controlled foreign corporations are taken from Lee Mahoney and Randy Miller, Controlled Foreign Corporations 2004, Internal Revenue Service *Statistics of Income Bulletin*, Summer 2008, (continued...)

---

as a reference point, are the remaining G-7 countries that are also among the United States' major trading partners. They account for 32% of pre-tax profits and 38% of rest-of-world gross domestic product. The second group of countries are larger countries from **Table 1** (with GDP of at least $10 billion), plus the Netherlands, which is widely considered a tax conduit for U.S. multinationals because of their holding company rules. These countries account for about 30% of earnings and 5% of rest-of-world GDP. The third group of countries are smaller countries listed in **Table 1**, with GDP less than $10 billion. These countries account for 14% of earnings and less than 1% of rest-of-world GDP.

As indicated in **Table 2**, income to GDP ratios in the large G-7 countries range from 0.2% to 2.6%, the latter reflecting in part the United States' relationships with some of its closest trading partners. Overall, this income as a share of GDP is 0.6%. Outside the United Kingdom and Canada, they are around 0.2% to 0.3% and do not vary with country size (Japan, for example, has over twice the GDP of Italy). Note also that Canada and the United Kingdom have also appeared on some tax haven lists and the larger income shares could partially reflect that.[48]

Table 2. U.S. Company Foreign Profits Relative to GDP, G-7, 2008

Country	Profits of U.S. Controlled Foreign Corporations as a Percentage of GDP
Canada	2.6
France	0.3
Germany	0.2
Italy	0.2
Japan	0.3
United Kingdom	1.3
Weighted Average	0.6

Source: CRS calculations, see text.

Table 3 reports the share for the larger tax havens listed in **Table 1** for which data are available, plus the Netherlands. In general, U.S. source profits as a percentage of GDP are considerably larger than those in **Table 2**. In the case of Luxembourg, these profits are 18% of output. Shares are also very large in Cyprus and Ireland. In all but two cases, the shares are well in excess of those in **Table 2**.

(...continued)

http://www.irs.ustreas.gov/pub/irs-soi/04coconfor.pdf. Data on GDP from Central Intelligence Agency, *The World Factbook*, https://www.cia.gov/library/publications/the-world-factbook. Most GDP data are for 2008 and based on the exchange rate but for some countries earlier years and data based on purchasing power parity were the only data available.

[48] One offshore website points out that Canada can be desirable as a place to establish a holding company; see Shelter Offshore,http://www.shelteroffshore.com/index.php/offshore/more/canada_offshore.

Table 3. U.S. Foreign Company Profits Relative to GDP, Larger Countries (GDP At Least $10 billion) on Tax Haven Lists and the Netherlands, 2008

Country	Profits of U.S. Controlled Corporations as a Percentage of GDP
Costa Rica	1.2
Cyprus	9.8
Hong Kong	2.8
Ireland	7.6
Luxembourg	18.2
Netherlands	4.6
Panama	3.0
Singapore	3.4
Switzerland	3.5
Taiwan	0.7

Source: CRS calculations, see text.

Table 4 examines the small tax havens listed in **Table 1** for which data are available. In three of the islands off the U.S. coast (in the Caribbean and Atlantic) profits are multiples of total GDP. Profits are well in excess of GDP in four jurisdictions. In other jurisdictions they are a large share of output. These numbers clearly indicate that the profits in these countries do not appear to derive from economic motives related to productive inputs or markets, but rather reflect income easily transferred to low-tax jurisdictions.

Table 4. U.S. Foreign Company Profits Relative to GDP, Small Countries on Tax Haven Lists, 2008

Country	Profits of U.S. Controlled Corporations as a Percentage of GDP
Bahamas	43.3
Barbados	13.2
Bermuda	645.7
British Virgin Islands	354.7
Cayman Islands	546.7
Guernsey	11.2
Jersey	35.3
Liberia	61.1
Malta	0.5
Marshall Islands	339.8
Mauritius	4.2
Netherland Antilles	8.9

Source: CRS calculations, see text.

Evidence of profit shifting has been presented in many other studies. Grubert and Altshuler report that profits of controlled foreign corporations in manufacturing relative to sales in Ireland are three times the group mean.[49] GAO reported higher shares of pretax profits of U.S. multinationals than of value added, tangible assets, sales, compensation or employees in low-tax countries such as Bermuda, Ireland, the UK Caribbean, Singapore, and Switzerland.[50] Costa and Gravelle reported similar results for tax havens using subsequent data.[51] Martin Sullivan reports the return on assets for 1998 averaged 8.4% for U.S. manufacturing subsidiaries, but with returns of 23.8% in Ireland, 17.9% in Switzerland, and 16.6% in the Cayman Islands.[52] More recently, he noted that of the 10 countries that accounted for the most foreign multinational profits, the five countries with the highest manufacturing returns for 2004 (the Netherlands, Bermuda, Ireland, Switzerland, and China) all had effective tax rates below 12% while the five countries with lower returns (Canada, Japan, Mexico, Australia, and the United Kingdom) had effective tax rates in excess of 23%.[53] A number of econometric studies of this issue have been done.[54]

Estimates of the Cost and Sources of Corporate Tax Avoidance

There are no official estimates of the cost of international corporate tax avoidance, although a number of researchers have made estimates, nor are there official estimates of the individual tax gap.[55] In general, the estimates are not reflected in the overall tax gap estimate. The magnitude of corporate tax avoidance has been estimated through a variety of techniques and not all are for total avoidance. Some address only avoidance by U.S. multinationals and not by foreign parents of U.S. subsidiaries. Some focus only on a particular source of avoidance.

Estimates of the potential revenue cost of income shifting by multinational corporations varies considerably, with estimates as high as $60 billion. The only study by the IRS in this area is an estimate of the international gross tax gap (not accounting for increased taxes collected on audit)

---

[49] Harry Grubert and Rosanne Altshuler, "Corporate Taxes in a World Economy: Reforming the Taxation of Cross-Border Income," in John W. Diamond and George Zodrow, eds., *Fundamental Tax Reform: Issues, Choices and Implications*, Cambridge, MIT Press, 2008.

[50] Government Accountability Office, *U.S. Multinational Corporations: Effective Tax Rates are Correlated With Where Income is Reported*, GAO-08-950, August 2008.

[51] Melissa Costa and Jennifer Gravelle, "U.S. Multinationals Business Activity: Effective Tax Rate and Location Decisions, National Tax Association Proceedings from the 103rd Annual Conference, 2010; http://www.ntanet.org/images/stories/pdf/proceedings/10/13.pdf.

[52] Martin Sullivan, U.S. Citizens Hide Hundreds of Billions in the Caymans, *Tax Notes*, May 24, 2004, p. 96.

[53] Martin Sullivan, "Extraordinary Profitability in Low-Tax Countries," *Tax Notes*, August 25, 2008, pp. 724-727. Note that the effective tax rates for some countries differ considerably depending on the source of data; the Netherlands would be classified as a low tax country based on data controlled foreign corporations but high tax based on BEA data. See Government Accountability Office, *U.S. Multinational Corporations: Effective Tax Rates are Correlated With Where Income is Reported*, GAO-08-950, August 2008.

[54] See James R. Hines, Jr., "Lessons from Behavioral Responses to International Taxation," *National Tax Journal*, vol. 52 (June 1999): 305-322, and Joint Committee on Taxation, *Economic Efficiency and Structural Analyses of Alternative U.S. Tax Policies for Foreign Direct Investment*, JCX-55-08, June 25, 2008, for reviews. Studies are also discussed in U.S. Department of Treasury, *The Deferral of Income of Earned Through Controlled Foreign Corporation*, May, 2000, http://www.treas.gov/offices/tax-policy/library/subpartf.pdf.

[55] This point is made by The Treasury Inspector General for Tax administration, "A Combination of Legislative Actions and Increased IRS Capability and Capacity are Required to Reduce the Multi-billion Dollar U.S. International Tax Gap," January 27 2009, 2009-I-R001.

---

related to transfer pricing based on audits of returns. They estimated a cost of about $3 billion, based on examinations of tax returns for 1996-1998.[56] This estimate would reflect an estimate not of legal avoidance, but of non-compliance, and for reasons stressed in the study has a number of limitations. One of those is that an audit does not detect all non-compliance, and it would not detect avoidance mechanisms which are, or appear to be, legal.

Some idea of the potential magnitude of the revenue lost from profit shifting by U.S. multinationals might be found in the estimates of the revenue gain from eliminating deferral. If most of the profit in low-tax countries has been shifted there to avoid U.S. tax rates, the projected revenue gain from ending deferral would provide an idea of the general magnitude of the revenue cost of profit shifting by U.S. parent firms. The Joint Committee on Taxation projects the revenue gain from ending deferral to be about $11 billion in FY2010.[57] This estimate could be either an overstatement or an understatement of the cost of tax avoidance. It could be an overstatement because some of the profits abroad accrue to real investments in countries that have lower tax rates than the United States and thus do not reflect artificial shifting. It could be an understatement because it does not reflect the tax that could be collected by the United States rather than foreign jurisdictions on profits shifted to low-tax countries. For example, Ireland has a tax rate of 12.5% and the United States a 35% rate, so that ending deferral (absent behavioral changes) would only collect the excess of the U.S. tax over the Irish tax on shifted revenues, or about two-thirds of lost revenue.

The Administration's estimates for ending deferral are slightly larger, over $14 billion.[58] Altshuler and Grubert estimate for 2002 that the corporate tax could be cut to 28% if deferral were ended, and based on corporate revenue in that year the gain is about $11 billion.[59] That year was at a low point because of the recession; if the share remained the same, the gain would be around $13 billion for 2004 and $26 billion for 2007. All of these estimates are based on tax data.

Researchers have looked at differences in pretax returns and estimated the revenue gain if returns were equated. This approach should provide some estimates of the magnitude of overall profit-shifting for multinationals, whether through transfer pricing, leveraging, or some other technique. Martin Sullivan, using Commerce Department data, estimates that, based on differences in pre-tax returns, the cost for 2004 was between $10 billion and $20 billion. Sullivan subsequently reports an estimated $17 billion increase in revenue loss from profit shifting between 1999 and 2004, which suggests that earlier number may be too small.[60] Sullivan suggests that the growth in

---

[56] U.S. Department of the Treasury, IRS, Report on the Application and Administration of Section 482, 1999.

[57] Joint Committee on Taxation, *Estimates of Federal Tax Expenditures for 2008-2012*, October 31, 2008.

[58] Budget for FY2010, *Analytical Perspectives*, p. 293.

[59] Harry Grubert and Rosanne Altshuler, "Corporate Taxes in the World Economy," in *Fundamental Tax Reform: Issues, Choices, and Implications* ed. John W. Diamond and George R. Zodrow, Cambridge, MIT Press, 2008.

[60] "Shifting Profits Offshore Costs U.S. Treasury $10 Billion or More," *Tax Notes*, September 27, 2004, pp. 1477-1481; "U.S. Multinationals Shifting Profits Out of the United States," *Tax Notes*, March 10, 2008, pp. 1078-1082. $75 billion in profits is artificially shifted abroad. If all of that income were subject to U.S. tax, it would result in a gain of $26 billion for 2004. Sullivan acknowledges that there are many difficulties in determining the revenue gain. Some of this income might already be taxed under Subpart F, some might be absorbed by excess foreign tax credits, and the effective tax rate may be lower than the statutory rate. Sullivan concludes that an estimate of between $10 billion and $20 billion is appropriate. Altshuler and Grubert suggest that Sullivan's methodology may involve some double counting; however, their own analysis finds that multinationals saved $7 billion more between 1997 and 2002 due to check the box rules. Some of this gain may have been at the cost of high-tax host countries rather than the United States, however. See Rosanne Altshuler and Harry Grubert, "Governments and Multinational Corporations in the Race to the Bottom," *Tax Notes International*, February 2006, pp. 459-474.

---

profit shifting may be due to check-the-box. Sullivan subsequently estimated a $28 billion loss for 2007 which he characterized as conservative.[61] Christian and Schultz, using rate of return on assets data from tax returns, estimated $87 billion was shifted in 2001, which, at a 35% tax rate, would imply a revenue loss of about $30 billion.[62] As a guide for potential revenue loss from avoidance, these estimates suffer from two limits. The first is the inability to determine how much was shifted out of high-tax foreign jurisdictions rather than the United States, which leads to a range of estimates. At the same time, if capital is mobile, economic theory indicates that the returns should be lower, the lower the tax rate. Thus the results could also understate the overall profit shifting and the revenue loss to the United States.

Pak and Zdanowicz examined export and import prices, and estimated that lost revenue due to transfer pricing of goods alone was $53 billion in 2001.[63] This estimate should cover both U.S. multinationals and U.S. subsidiaries of foreign parents, but is limited to one technique. Clausing, using regression techniques on cross-country data, which estimated profits reported as a function of tax rates, estimated that revenues of over $60 billion are lost for 2004 by applying a 35% tax rate to an estimated $180 billion in corporate profits shifted out of the United States.[64] She estimates that the profit shifting effects are twice as large as the effects from shifts in actual economic activity. This methodological approach differs from others which involve direct calculations based on returns or prices and is subject to the econometric limitations with cross-country panel regressions. In theory, however, it had an overall of coverage of shifting (that is both outbound by U.S. parents of foreign corporations and inbound by foreign parents of U.S. corporations and covering all techniques).

Clausing and Avi-Yonah estimate the revenue gain from moving to a formula apportionment based on sales that is on the order of $50 billion per year because the fraction of worldwide income in the United States is smaller than the fraction of worldwide sales.[65] While this estimate is not an estimate of the loss from profit shifting (since sales and income could differ for other reasons), it is suggestive of the magnitude of total effects from profit shifting. A similar result was found by another study that applied formula apportionment based on an equal weight of assets, payroll, and sales.[66]

A more recent study by Clausing indicated that the revenue loss from profit shifting profit shifting may be as high as $90 billion in 2008, although an alternative data set indicates profit shifting of

---

[61] Martin Sullivan, "Transfer Pricing Costs U.S. At Least $28 Billion," *Tax Notes*, March 22, 2010, pp. 1439-1443.

[62] Charles W. Christian and Thomas D. Schultz, ROA-Based Estimates of Income Shifting by Multinational Corporations, *IRS Research Bulletin*, 2005 http://www.irs.gov/pub/irs-soi/05christian.pdf.

[63] Simon J. Pak and John S. Zdanowicz, *U.S. Trade With the World, An Estimate of 2001 Lost U.S. Federal Income Tax Revenues Due to Over-Invoiced Imports and Under-Invoiced Exports,* October 31, 2002.

[64] Kimberly Clausing, Multinational Firm Tax Avoidance and Tax Policy, *National Tax Journal*, vol. 62, December 2009, pp. 703-725, Working Paper, March 2008. Her method involved estimating the profit differentials as a function of tax rate differentials over the period 1982-2004 and then applying that coefficient to current earnings.

[65] Kimberly A. Clausing and Reuven S. Avi-Yonah, *Reforming Corporate Taxation in a Global Economy: A Proposal to Adopt Formulary Apportionment*, Brookings Institution: The Hamilton Project, Discussion paper 2007-2008, June 2007.

[66] Douglas Shackelford and Joel Slemrod, "The Revenue Consequences of Using Formula apportionment to Calculate U.S. and Foreign Source Income: A Firm Level Analysis," *International Tax and Public Finance*, vol. 5, no. 1, 1998, pp. 41-57.

$57 billion.[67] For the last five years, the first method yielded losses ranging from 20% to 30% of profits. Using the second method, the range was 13% to 20%.

It is very difficult to develop a separate estimate for U.S. subsidiaries of foreign multinational companies because there is no way to observe the parent firm and its other subsidiaries. Several studies have documented that these firms have lower taxable income and that some have higher debt to asset ratios than domestic firms. There are many other potential explanations these differing characteristics, however, and domestic firms that are used as comparisons also have incentives to shift profits when they have foreign operations. No quantitative estimate has been made.[68] However some evidence of earnings stripping for inverted firms was found.[69]

Importance of Different Profit Shifting Techniques

Some studies have attempted to identify the importance of techniques used for profit shifting. Grubert has estimated that about half of income shifting was due to transfer pricing of intangibles and most of the remainder to shifting of debt.[70] In a subsequent study, Altshuler and Grubert find that multinationals saved $7 billion more between 1997 and 2002 due to check the box rules.[71] Some of this gain may have been at the cost of high-tax host countries rather than the United States, however.

Some of the estimates discussed here conflict with respect to the source of profit shifting. The Pak and Zdanowich estimates suggest that transfer pricing of goods is an important mechanism of tax avoidance, while Grubert suggests that the main methods of profit shifting are due to leverage and intangibles. The estimates for pricing of goods may, however, reflect errors, or money laundering motives rather than tax motives. Much of the shifting was associated with trade with high-tax countries; for example, Japan, Canada, and Germany accounted for 18% of the total.[72] At the same time, about 14% of the estimate reflected transactions with countries that appear on tax haven lists: the Netherlands, Taiwan, Singapore, Hong Kong, and Ireland.

---

[67] Kimberly A. Clausing, "The Revenue Effects of Multinational Firm Income Shifting," Tax Notes, March 28, 2011, pp. 1580-1586.

[68] These studies are discussed and new research presented in U.S. Department of Treasury, *Report to Congress on Earnings Stripping, Transfer Pricing and U.S. Income Tax Treaties*, November 2007. One study used a different approach, examining taxes of firms before and after acquisition by foreign versus domestic acquirers, but the problem of comparison remains and the sample was very small; that study found no differences. See Jennifer L. Blouin, Julie H. Collins, and Douglas A. Shackelford, "Does Acquisition by Non-U.S. Shareholders Cause U.S. firms to Pay Less Tax?" *Journal of the American Taxation Association*, Spring 2008, pp. 25-38. Harry Grubert, *Debt and the Profitability of Foreign Controlled Domestic Corporations in the United States*, Office of Tax Analysis Technical Working Paper No. 1, July 2008, http://www.ustreas.gov/offices/tax-policy/library/otapapers/otatech2008.shtml#2008.

[69] In addition to the 2007 Treasury study cited above, see Jim A. Seida and William F. Wempe, "Effective Tax Rate Changes and Earnings Stripping Following Corporate Inversion," *National Tax Journal*, vol. 57, December 2007, pp. 805-828. They estimated $0.7 billion of revenue loss from four firms that inverted. Inverted firms may, however, behave differently from foreign firms with U.S. subsidiaries.

[70] Harry Grubert, "Intangible Income, Intercompany Transactions, Income Shifting, and the Choice of Location," *National Tax Journal*, Vo. 56,March 2003, Part 2.

[71] Rosanne Altshuler and Harry Grubert, "Governments and Multinational Corporations in the Race to the Bottom," *Tax Notes International*, February 2006, pp. 459-474.

[72] Data are presented in "Who's Watching our Back Door?" *Business Accents*, Florida International University, Fall 2004, pp. 26-29.

Some evidence that points to the importance of intangibles and the associated profits in tax haven countries can be developed by examining the sources of dividends repatriated during the "repatriation holiday" enacted in 2004.[73] This provision allowed, for a temporary period, dividends to be repatriated with an 85% deduction, leading to a tax rate of 5.25%. The pharmaceutical and medicine industry accounted for $99 billion in repatriations or 32% of the total. The computer and electronic equipment industry accounted for $58 billion or 18% of the total. Thus these two industries, which are high tech firms, accounted for half of the repatriations. The benefits were also highly concentrated in a few firms. According to a recent study, five firms (Pfizer, Merck, Hewlett-Packard, Johnson & Johnson, and IBM) are responsible for $88 billion, over a quarter (28%) of total repatriations.[74] The top 10 firms (adding Schering-Plough, Du Pont, Bristol-Myers Squibb, Eli Lilly, and PepsiCo) accounted for 42%. The top 15 (adding Procter and Gamble, Intel, Coca-Cola, Altria, and Motorola) accounted for over half (52%). These are firms that tend to, in most cases, have intangibles either in technology or brand names.

Finally, as shown in **Table 5**, which lists all countries accounting for at least 1% of the total of eligible dividends (and accounting for 87% of the total), most of the dividends were repatriated from countries that appear on tax haven lists.

Table 5. Source of Dividends from "Repatriation Holiday":
Countries Accounting for At Least 1% of Dividends

Country	Percentage of Total
Netherlands	28.8
Switzerland	10.4
Bermuda	10.2
Ireland	8.2
Luxembourg	7.5
Canada	5.9
Cayman Islands	5.9
United Kingdom	5.1
Hong Kong	1.7
Singapore	1.7
Malaysia	1.2

Source: Internal Revenue Service.

Methods of Avoidance and Evasion by Individuals

Individual evasion of taxes may take different forms, and they are all facilitated by the growing international financial globalization and ease of making transactions on the Internet. Individuals

---

[73] Data are taken from Melissa Redmiles, "The One-Time Dividends-Received Deduction," Internal Revenue Service *Statistics of Income Bulletin*, spring 2008, http://www.irs.ustreas.gov/pub/irs-soi/08codivdeductbul.pdf.

[74] Rodney P. Mock and Andreas Simon, "Permanently Reinvested Earnings: Priceless," *Tax Notes*, November 17, 2008, pp. 835-848.

can purchase foreign investments directly (outside the United States), such as stocks and bonds, or put money in foreign bank accounts and simply not report the income (although it is subject to tax under U.S. tax law). There is little or no withholding information on individual taxpayers for this type of action. They can also use structures such as trusts or shell corporations to evade tax on investments, including investments made in the United States, which may take advantage of U.S. tax laws that exempt interest income and capital gains of non-residents from U.S. tax. Rather than using withholding or information collection the United States largely relies on the Qualified Intermediary (QI) program where beneficial owners are not revealed. To the extent any information gathering from other countries is done it is through bilateral information exchanges rather than multilateral information sharing. The European Union has developed a multilateral agreement but the United States does not participate.

Tax Provisions Affecting the Treatment of Income by Individuals

The ability of U.S. persons (whether firms or individuals) to avoid tax on U.S. source income that they would normally be subject to arises from U.S. rules that do not impose withholding taxes on many sources of income. In general interest and capital gains are not subject to withholding. Dividends, non-portfolio interest (such as interest payments by a U.S. subsidiary to its parent), capital gains connected with a trade or business, and certain rents are subject to tax, although treaty arrangements widely reduce or eliminate the tax on dividends. In addition, even when dividends are potentially subject to a withholding tax, new techniques have developed to transform, through derivatives, those assets into exempt interest.[75]

The elimination of tax on interest income was unilaterally initiated by the United States in 1984, and other countries began to follow suit.[76] Currently, fears of capital flight are likely to keep countries from changing this treatment. However, it has been accompanied with a lack of information reporting and lack of information sharing that allows U.S. citizens, who are liable for these taxes, to avoid them whether on income invested abroad or income invested in the United States channeled through shell corporations and trusts. Citizens of foreign countries can also evade the tax, and the U.S. practice of not collecting information contributes to the problem.

Based on actual tax cases, Guttenberg and Avi-Yonah describe a typical way that U.S. individuals can easily evade tax on domestic income through a Cayman Islands operation with little expense using current technology. The individual, using the Internet, can open a bank account in the name of a Cayman corporation that can be set up for a minimal fee. Money can be electronically transferred without any reporting to tax authorities, and investments can be made in the United States or abroad. Investments by non-residents in interest bearing assets and most capital gains are not subject to a withholding tax in the United States.[77]

In addition to corporations, foreign trusts can be used to accomplish the same approach. Trusts may involve a trust protector who is an intermediary between the grantor and the trustees, but whose purpose may actually be to carry out the desires of the grantor. Some taxpayers argue that

---

[75] See Joint Committee on *Taxation Tax Compliance and Enforcement Issues With Respect to Offshore Entities and Accounts*, JCX-23-09, March 30, 2009, p. 6 for a discussion.

[76] This history is described by Reuven Avi-Yonah in testimony before the Committee on Select Revenue Measures of the Ways and Means Committee, March 5, 2008.

[77] Joseph Guttentag and Reven Avi-Yonah, "Closing the International Tax Gap," in Max B. Sawicky, ed. *Bridging the Tax Gap: Addressing the Crisis in Federal Tax Administration*, Washington, D.C., Economic Policy Institute, 2005.

these trusts are legal but in either case they can be used to protect income from taxes, including those invested in the United States, from tax, while retaining control over and use of the funds.

Limited Information Reporting Between Jurisdictions

In general, the international taxation of passive portfolio income by individuals is easily subject to evasion because there is no multilateral reporting of interest income. Even in those cases where bilateral information sharing treaties, referred to as Tax Information Exchange Agreements (TIEAs) are in place, they have limits. As pointed out by Avi-Yonah most of these agreements are restricted to criminal matters, which are a minor part of the revenues involved and pose difficult issues of evidence. Also, these agreements sometimes require that the activities related to the information being sought constitute crimes in both countries which can be a substantial hurdle in cases of tax evasion. The OECD has adopted a model agreement with the "dual criminality" requirements.[78] TIEAs usually allow for information only upon request, requiring the United States and other countries to identify the potential tax evaders in advance and they do not override bank secrecy laws.

In some cases the countries themselves have little or no information of value. One article, for example, discussing the possibility of an information exchange agreement with the British Virgin Islands, a country with more than 400,000 registered corporations, where laws require no identification of shareholders or directors, and require no financial records, noted: "Even if the BVI signs an information exchange agreement, it is not clear what information could be exchanged."[79]

U.S. Collection of Information on U.S. Income and Qualified Intermediaries

Under the QI program the United States itself does not require U.S. financial institutions to identify the true beneficiaries of interest and exempt dividends. The IRS has set up a QI program in 2001, under which foreign banks that received payments certify the nationality of their depositors and reveal the identity of any U.S. citizens.[80] However, although QIs are supposed to certify nationality,[81] apparently some rely on self certification.[82] They are also subject to audit. However, UBS, the Swiss bank involved in a tax abuse scandal that helped clients set up offshore plans, was a QI, and that event has raised some questions about the QI program.

A non-qualified intermediary must disclose the identity of its customers to obtain the exemption for passive income such as interest and or the reduced rates arising from tax treaties, but there are also questions about the accuracy of disclosures.

---

[78] Testimony of Reuven Avi-Yonah, Subcommittee on Select Revenue Measures, Ways and Means Committee, March 31, 2009.

[79] "Brown Pushes U.K. Tax havens On OECD Standards" *Tax Notes International*, April 20, 2009, pp. 180-181.

[80] A very clear and brief explanation of the origin of the QI program and of the requirements can be found in Martin Sullivan, "Proposals to Fight Offshore Tax Evasion," *Tax Notes*, April 20, 2009, pp. 264-268.

[81] For additional discussion of the QI program, see Joint Committee on Taxation, *Tax Compliance and Enforcement Issues With Respect to Offshore Entities and Accounts*, JCX-23-09, March 30, 2009.

[82] Martin A. Sullivan, "Proposals to Fight Offshore Tax Evasion," *Tax Notes*, April 20, 2009.

The HIRE Act, P.L. 111-147, included some provisions strengthening the rules affecting qualified intermediaries, although the projected revenue gain was quite small (less than $1 billion per year) relative to projected costs (discussed below).

European Union Savings Directive

The European Union, in its savings directive, has developed among its members an option of either information reporting or a withholding tax. The reporting or withholding option covers the member countries as well as some other countries. Three states, Austria, Belgium, and Luxembourg, have elected the withholding tax. While this multilateral agreement aids these countries' tax administration, the United States is not a participant.

Estimates of the Revenue Cost of Individual Tax Evasion

A number of different approaches have been used to estimate corporate tax avoidance, however, all of these approaches rely on data reported on assets and income. For individual evasion, estimates are much more difficult because the initial basis of the estimate is the amount of assets held abroad whose income is not reported to the tax authorities. In addition to this estimate, the expected rate of return and tax rate are needed to estimate the revenue cost.

Guttentag and Avi-Yonah estimate a value of $50 billion in individual tax evasion, based on an estimate of holdings by high net worth individuals invested outside the United States at $1.5 trillion.[83] Using a rate of return of 10% and a tax rate of approximately one-third, they obtain an estimate of $50 billion. They also summarize two other estimates in 2002 of $40 billion for the international tax gap by the IRS and $70 billion by an IRS consultant.

To the extent that the earnings are interest, the 10% rate of return may be too high, while if it is dividends and capital gains, the tax rate is too high. Using a tax rate of 15% (currently applicable to capital gains and dividends) would lead to about $23 billion. In the case of equity investments, if a third of the return is in dividends and half of capital gains is never realized, the tax rate would be 10% or about $15 billion assuming the 10% return. During 2002 and beginning in 2011, however, the tax rate on capital gains and dividends is 20%, indicating a loss of $20 billion rather than $15 billion. For interest, since investors can earn tax free returns in the neighborhood of 4% to 5% on domestic state and local bonds, to yield a 5% after-tax return at a 35% tax rate would require a pre-tax yield of about 7.7%. The estimate would then be $40 billion.

The Tax Justice Network has estimated a worldwide revenue loss for all countries of $255 billion from individual tax evasion, basically using a 7.5% return and a 30% tax rate.[84] These assumptions would be consistent with a $33 billion loss for the United States using the $1.5 trillion figure. Their worldwide numbers are consistent with $11 trillion in offshore wealth. Their more recent estimates place wealth at $21 trillion to $32 trillion, which would double or triple

---

[83] Joseph Guttentag and Reven Avi-Yonah, "Closing the International Tax Gap," in Max B. Sawicky, ed. *Bridging the Tax Gap: Addressing the Crisis in Federal Tax Administration*, Washington, D.C., Economic Policy Institute, 2005.

[84] Tax Justice Network, *Tax Us If You Can,* September, 2005.

these estimates.[85] Thus the cost for the United States could be much larger approaching $100 billion.

Alternative Policy Options to Address Corporate Profit Shifting

Because much of the corporate tax revenue loss arises from activities that either are legal or appear to be so, it is difficult to address these issues other than with changes in the tax law. Outcomes would likely be better if there is international cooperation. Currently, the possibilities for international cooperation appear to play a bigger role in options for dealing with individual evasion than with corporate avoidance.

Broad Changes to International Tax Rules

The first set of provisions would introduce broad changes in international tax rules, and include significant restrictions in deferral or allocation of income and capital.

Repeal Deferral

One approach to mitigate the rewards of profit shifting is to repeal deferral, or to institute true worldwide taxation of foreign source income. Firms would be subject to current tax on the income of their foreign subsidiaries, although they would continue to be able to take foreign tax credits. According to estimates cited above, this change currently would raise from $11 billion to $14 billion per year.

Many of the issues surrounding the repeal of deferral have focused on the real effects of repeal on the allocation of capital. Traditionally, economic analysis has suggested that eliminating deferral would increase economic efficiency, although recently some have argued that this gain would be offset by the loss of production of some efficient firms from high-tax countries. Some have also argued for retaining the current system or moving in the other direction to a territorial tax. These economic issues are discussed in detail in another CRS report.[86]

Repeal of deferral would largely eliminate the value of the planning techniques discussed in this report. There are concerns, however, that firms could avoid the effects of repeal by having their parent incorporate in other countries that continue to allow deferral. The most direct and beneficial to reducing firms' tax liabilities of these planning approaches, inversion, has been addressed by legislation in 2004.[87] Mergers would be another method to counter the implementation of deferral, although mergers involve real changes in organization that would not likely be undertaken to gain a small tax benefit. Another possibility is that more direct portfolio investment (i.e., buying shares of stock by individual investors) in foreign corporations will

[85]Tax Justice Network, *Estimating the Price of Offshore*, July22, 2012, at http://www.taxjustice.net/cms/front_content.php?idcat=148.

[86] CRS Report RL34115, *Reform of U.S. International Taxation: Alternatives*, by Jane G. Gravelle.

[87] Firms with 80% continuity of ownership would be treated as U.S. firms and firms with at least 60% continuity of ownership would be subject to tax on the transfer of assets for the next 10 years.

occur. There has been a significant growth in this direct investment, although the evidence suggests this investment has been due to portfolio diversification and not tax avoidance.[88]

S. 3018, a broad tax reform bill introduced by Senators Wyden and Gregg, would eliminate deferral.

Targeted or Partial Elimination of Deferral

More narrow proposals to address deferral and tax avoidance would tax income in tax havens currently, or tax some additional income of foreign subsidiaries. They include

- eliminating deferral for specified tax havens,
- eliminating deferral in countries with tax rates that are below the U.S. rate by a specified proportion,
- eliminating deferral for income on the production of goods that are in turn imported into the United States,
- eliminate deferral for income on the production of goods that are exported, and
- requiring a minimum payout share.

Restricting current taxation to tax havens would likely address some of the problems associated with transfer pricing and leveraging, without ending deferral entirely. Defining a tax haven under those circumstances would be crucial. A bill introduced in the 110th Congress, S. 396, which defined as a U.S. firm any U.S. subsidiary in a tax haven not engaged in an active business, had a list of countries that was the same as the original OECD tax haven list, except for the U.S. Virgin Islands. Some countries that are often considered tax havens, would not be subject to such provisions, leaving some scope for corporate tax avoidance. In addition, firms could shift some operations to other lower tax countries and increase the amount of foreign tax credits available, which would be a loss to U.S. revenue. Some concerns have also been expressed that listing specific tax haven countries would make cooperative approaches, such as tax information sharing treaties, more difficult.

An alternative, which would not require identifying particular countries, would be to restrict deferral based on a tax rate that is lower than the U.S. rate by a specified amount. For example, the French, who generally have a territorial tax, tax income earned in jurisdictions with tax rates one-third lower than the French rate. For the United States, whose tax rate is similar to the French rate, this ratio would indicate a tax rate lower than 24%.

Another proposal directed to "runaway" plans would eliminate deferral for investments abroad that produce exports into the United States. S. 1284, also in the 110th Congress, would impose current taxation on such activities by expanding Subpart F income to include income attributable to imports into the United States of goods produced by foreign subsidiaries of U.S. firms. The main problem with this proposal is administering it, which would include tracing selling to a third party for resale.

---

[88] See CRS Report RL34115, *Reform of U.S. International Taxation: Alternatives*, by Jane G. Gravelle. See also International Corporate Tax Reform Proposals: Issues and Proposals, Forthcoming, *Florida Tax Review*, by Jane G. Gravelle.

A somewhat different and more restrictive proposal was made by Senator Kerry during the 2004 presidential campaign. He proposed to eliminate deferral except in the case where income is produced and sold in the controlled foreign corporation's (CFC's) jurisdiction. This approach would, like deferral in general, be likely to significantly restrict opportunities for artificial profit shifting, since most of the income in tax haven or low-tax jurisdictions do not arise from real activity; indeed, these jurisdictions are too small in many cases to provide a market. As with the previous proposal, however, the administration of such a plan would be difficult.

A final option that would not go as far as eliminating deferral altogether would be to require some minimum share to be paid out.

Allocation of Deductions and Credits with Respect to Deferred Income/Restrictions on Cross Crediting

A proposal that does not end deferral but makes the shifting of profits from high-tax countries less attractive is a provision to allocate deductions and credits, so as to deny those benefits until income is repatriated. This approach was included in a tax reform bill introduced by Chairman Rangel of the Ways and Means Committee in 2007 (H.R. 3970) and is included in the current proposals by President Obama. Under this proposal, a portion of certain overall deductions, such as interest or overhead, that reflects the share of foreign deferred income, would be disallowed. The foreign tax credit allocation rule would allow credits for the share of foreign taxes paid that is equal to the share of foreign source income repatriated. Disallowed deductions and credits would be carried forward. (President Obama's proposal does not allocate research and experimental expenses.)

The allocation-of-deductions provision would decrease the tax benefits of sheltering income in low-tax jurisdictions and encourage repatriation of income relative to current law and presumably reduce profit shifting, as well as decreasing benefits of real investment abroad. The foreign tax credit allocation rule could have a variety of effects. It would make foreign investment abroad less attractive because it would increase the tax on income when eventually repatriated, it would discourage investment in low-tax jurisdictions that could no longer be sheltered by foreign tax credits, and it would discourage repatriation of earnings on existing activities because of the potential tax to be collected.

The allocation of credits accomplishes some of the restrictions on cross crediting that could also be achieved by increasing the number of baskets. As discussed below, one possible separate basket would be for active royalties. Another possibility would be to impose a per country limit with a separate basket for each country (and baskets within each for passive, active, etc., income). S. 3018, a broad tax reform bill introduced by Senators Wyden and Gregg, would provide for a per country limit.

Formula Apportionment

Another approach to addressing income shifting is through formula apportionment, which would be a major change in the international tax system. With formula apportionment, income would be allocated to different jurisdictions based on their shares of some combination of sales, assets, and employment. This approach is used by many states in the United States and by the Canadian provinces to allocate income. (In the past, a three factor apportionment was used, but some states have moved to a sales based system.) Studies have estimated a significant increase in taxes from adopting formula apportionment. Slemrod and Shackleford estimate a 38% revenue increase from an equally weighted three-factor system.[89] A sales-based formula has been proposed by Avi-Yonah and Clausing that they estimate would raise about 35% of additional corporate revenue, or $50 billion annually over the 2001-2004 period.[90]

The ability of a formula apportionment system to address some of the problems of shifting income becomes problematic with intangible assets.[91] If all capital were tangible capital, such as buildings and equipment, a formula apportionment system based on capital would at least lead to the same rate of return for tax purposes across high-tax and low-tax jurisdictions. Real distortions in the allocation of capital would remain, since capital would still flow to low-tax jurisdictions, but paper profits could not be shifted. An allocation system based on assets becomes more difficult when intangible assets are involved. It is probably as difficult to estimate the stock of intangible investment (given lack of information on the future pattern of profitability) as it is to allocate it under arms-length pricing. In the case of an allocation based on sales, profits that might appropriately be associated with domestic income as they arise from domestic investment in R&D would be allocated abroad. Moreover, new avenues of tax planning, such as selling to an intermediary in a low-tax country for resale, would complicate the administration of such a plan. Whether the benefits are greater than the costs is in some dispute.

One problem is that if the United States adopted the system there could be double taxation of some income and no taxation of other income unless there were a multinational plan. The European Union has been considering a formula apportionment, based on property, gross receipts, number of employees and cost of employment. This proposal and the consequences for different countries are discussed by Devereux and Loretz.[92] If the European Union adopted such a plan it would be easier for the United States to adopt a similar apportionment formula without as much risk of double or no taxation with respect to its major trading partners.

Eliminate Check the Box, Hybrid Entities, and Hybrid Instruments; Foreign Tax Credit Splitting From Income

A number of proposals have been made to eliminate check the box, and in general to adopt rules that would require that legal entities be characterized in a consistent manner by the United States and the country where the entity is established. This proposal has been made by McIntyre.[93] In general rules to require that legal entities be characterized in a consistent manner by the United States and by the country where established and that tax benefits that arise from inconsistent

---

[89] Douglas Shackelford and Joel Slemrod, "The Revenue Consequences of Using Formula apportionment to Calculate U.S. and Foreign Source Income: A Firm Level Analysis," *International Tax and Public Finance*, vol. 5, no. 1, 1998, pp. 41-57.

[90] Kimberly A. Clausing and Reuven A. Avi-Yonah, *Reforming Corporate Taxation in a Global Economy : A Proposal to Adopt Formulary Apportionment*, Brookings Institution: The Hamilton Project, Discussion paper 2007-08, June 2007.

[91] These and other issues are discussed by Rosanne Altshuler and Harry Grubert, "Formula Apportionment: Is it Better than the Current System and Are There Better Alternatives?" Oxford University Centre for Business Taxation, Working paper 09/01.

[92] Michael P. Devereux and Simon Loretz, "The Effects of EU formula Apportionment on Corporate Tax Revenues," *Fiscal Studies*, Vol. 29, no. 1, pp. 1-33. http://www3.interscience.wiley.com/cgi-bin/fulltext/119399105/PDFSTART? CRETRY=1&SRETRY=0.

[93] Michael McIntyre, "A Program for International Tax Reform," *Tax Notes*, February 23, 2009, pp. 1021-1026.

---

treatment of instruments be denied would address this particular class of provisions that undermine Subpart F and the matching of credits and deductions with income. President Obama's proposal includes a provision that disallows a subsidiary to treat a subsidiary chartered in another country as a disregarded entity. It also includes a provision to prevent foreign tax credits without the associated income, which can currently be accomplished with reverse hybrids. This provision is included in H.R. 4213, the American Jobs and Closing Loopholes Act, passed by the House.

Narrower Provisions Affecting Multinational Profit Shifting

A number of more narrow provisions could be considered that would be more focused on preventing abuses and have fewer consequences for the overall structure of international corporate taxation.

Tighten Earnings Stripping Rules

In the American Jobs Creation Act a further restriction on earnings stripping rules was considered as an alternative to the anti-inversion measure. These provisions were not enacted, but were to be studied in a Treasury report. The 2004 House proposal would have raised revenue by dropping the debt to asset share test and lowering the interest share standard to 25% for ordinary debt, 50% for guaranteed debt, and 30% overall. In general, further restrictions on earnings stripping could be considered to address shifting through debt for U.S. subsidiaries of foreign parents.

President Obama's plan includes dropping the asset test and lowering the interest share standard to 25% for inverted firms, with respect to related party non-guaranteed debt.

Foreign Tax Credits: Source Royalties as Domestic Income for Purposes of the Foreign Tax Credit Limit, Or Create Separate Basket; Eliminate Title Passage Rule; Restrict Credits for Taxes Producing an Economic Benefit; Address Specific Techniques for Enhancing Foreign Tax Credits

As noted above, one of the issues surrounding the cross-crediting of the foreign tax credit is the use of excess credits to shield royalties from U.S. tax on income that could be considered U.S. source income. Two options might be considered to address that issue: sourcing these royalties as domestic income for purposes of the credit or putting them into a separate foreign tax credit basket.[94] The same issue applies to the provision that allows half of the income from exports to be allocated to the country in which the title passes. President Obama's proposal includes a provision to restrict the crediting of taxes that are in exchange for an economic benefit (such as payments that are the equivalent of royalties).

H.R. 4213, the American Jobs and Closing Loopholes Act, passed by the House, would address a number of specialized techniques for increasing foreign tax credits.

---

[94] Harry Grubert, "Tax Credits, Source Rules, Trade and Electronic Commerce: Behavioral Margins and the Design of International Tax Systems," *Tax Law Review*, vol. 58, January 2005; also issued as CESIFO Working Paper no. 1366, December 2004.; Harry Grubert and Rosanne Altshuler, "Corporate Taxes in a World Economy: Reforming the Taxation of Cross-Border Income," in John W. Diamond and George Zodrow, eds., *Fundamental Tax Reform: Issues, Choices and Implications*, Cambridge, MIT Press, 2008.

Transfer Pricing

Michael McIntyre has suggested some other proposals to deal with transfer pricing, which include making transfer pricing penalties nearly automatic for taxpayers who have not kept contemporaneous records. He also suggests use of some type of formula apportionment plan as a default for transfer pricing for non-complying taxpayers so the IRS does not have to conduct a detailed transaction by transaction assessment for the court.

President Obama's proposals would address some of the transfer pricing issues associated with the transfer of intangibles by clarifying that intangibles include workforce in place, goodwill, and going concern value and that they are valued at their highest and best use. The plan would allow the IRS Commissioner to aggregate intangibles if that leads to a more appropriate value.

These proposals would likely have small effects. Any significant solution to the transfer pricing problem, especially for intangibles, is difficult to entertain short of an elimination of deferral.

The President's FY2011 budget proposal included a plan to treat excess returns on intangibles in a low-tax country as Subpart F income (and therefore not subject to deferral) and to place it in a separate foreign tax-credit basket. If such an approach could be successfully implemented it might have important consequences for transfer pricing using intangibles.

Codify Economic Substance Doctrine (Enacted Provision)

The economic substance doctrine was recently adopted in the health reform legislation, P.L. 111-148. This provision is relevant to international tax evasion and avoidance. Firms that enter into tax savings arrangements that are found not to have economic substance can have their tax benefits disallowed by the courts under what has become known as the economic substance doctrine. The doctrine is sometimes interpreted differently by different courts and recent legislative proposals have sought to make the doctrine more uniform through statute. Generally these proposals would require a transaction to meet both an objective test (profit was made) and a subjective test (profit was intended). Penalties are also imposed. Supporters argue that the stricter test will not only reduce tax avoidance but also make treatment more consistent across the courts. Some tax attorneys are concerned that more specific rules might provide a roadmap to structuring arrangements that will pass the test. The provision adopted in P.L. 111-148 included a two-part statutory standard.

Prevent Dividend Repatriation Through Reorganizations (Boot Within Gain)

President Obama's plan would revise the rule on reorganizations when property as well as stock is received to treat distributions as dividends in the case of cross-border transactions, and this provision is included in H.R. 4213, the American Jobs and Closing Loopholes Act, passed by the House.

Options to Address Individual Evasion

Most of the options for addressing individual evasion involve more information reporting and additional enforcement. There are options that would involve fundamental changes in the law, such as shifting from a residence to a source basis for passive income. That is, the United States would tax this passive income earned in its borders, just as is the case for corporate and other active income. This change involves, however, many other economic and efficiency effects that are probably not desirable. The remainder of the proposals discussed here do not involve any fundamental changes in the tax itself, but rather focus on administration and enforcement.

The options discussed below are drawn from many sources, including academics and practitioners, organizations, and the Internal Revenue Service, and contained in legislative proposals; citations to these sources are provided at this point and legislative proposals are summarized in the next section.[95]

Some of the options discussed in this section are included in the HIRE Act, P.L. 111-147, and that inclusion will be noted.

Information Reporting

Expanded information reporting can involve multilateral efforts, changes in the current bilateral treaties, or unilateral changes.

Multilateral Information Sharing or Withholding; International Cooperation

The option that appears likely to recover most of the revenues would be to join in the European Union Directive, which would require information reporting on all income paid to foreign entities by U.S. banks and other institutions. If the beneficial owner cannot be identified, withholding could be imposed (a refund would be allowed if evidence of reporting to the home country could be shown). This approach has been proposed by the Tax Justice Network, which also suggests expanding the treaty to other tax havens. If the European Union is receptive, it would benefit other countries by reporting income paid to foreign nationals and benefit the United States by achieving third party information reporting on foreign investments of U.S. citizens.

Avi-Yonah and Avi-Yonah and Guttentag have suggested that current Treasury policy is to focus on bilateral agreements to achieve information exchange, but that the United States should also focus on cooperation with the OECD and G-20 and other appropriate organizations to improve information and persuade tax havens to enter into exchanges based on the OECD model. Shay suggests this approach as well and particularly references electronic information exchange.

The Tax Justice Network has proposed that the United Nations develop a global tax cooperation standard, set up a panel to determine compliant states, and deny recognition to non-compliant jurisdictions. They have also suggested that the IMF and World Bank country assessments address tax compliance.

---

[95]For discussions of various proposals listed see Tax Justice Network, "Ending the Offshore Secrecy System," March 2009, http://www.taxjustice.net/cms/upload/pdf/TJN_0903_Action_Plan_for_G-20.pdf ; testimony of Reuven Avi-Yonah, Peter Blessing, Stephen Shay, and Douglas Shulman before the Subcommittee on Select Revenue Measures of the Ways and Means Committee, March 31, 2009; Martin Sullivan, "Proposals to Fight Offshore Tax Evasion," *Tax Notes*, part 1, April 20, 2009, pp. 264-268; part 2: April 27, 2009, pp. 371-373; part 3, May 4, 2009, pp. 516-520; Reuven Avi-Yonah, Testimony before the Committee on Select Revenue Measures of the Ways and Means Committee, March 5, 2008; Testimony of Jack A. Blum and, Testimony on the Cayman Islands and Offshore Tax Issues before the Senate finance Committee, July 24, 2008; Michael McIntyre, "A Program for International Tax Reform," *Tax Notes*, February 23, 2009, pp. 1021-1026.

Expanding Bilateral Information Exchange

A number of commentators have suggested an increase in the scope of bilateral information treaties to provide for regular and automatic exchanges of information. This would require the U.S. banks to increase their collection of information.

Avi-Yonah and Avid-Yonah and Guttentag suggest adopting the model OECD bilateral Tax Information Exchange Agreement (TIEA). This information exchange would relate to civil as well as criminal issues, it would not require suspicion of a crime other than tax evasion, and would override tax haven bank secrecy laws. Non-tax havens could be induced to make such agreements to obtain information, and thus, such a change would require collection of information on interest payments by banks and financial institutions. Treasury has proposed only 16 countries, but Avi-Yonah and Guttenberg suggest no reason to restrict the provision in this way. Treasury could use existing authority not to exchange information that might be misused by non-democratic foreign governments.

Martin Sullivan suggests that automatic information exchange might be the only way to stop evasion, which would require renegotiating existing agreements and a major policy change. He notes that that the proposed Stop Tax Haven Abuse Act (S. 506, H.R. 1265) requires automatic information exchange for a country to stay off the tax haven list.

Unilateral Approaches: Withholding/Refund Approach; Increased Information Reporting Requirements

This step is one that the United States could undertake without multilateral or bilateral cooperation, namely imposing withholding taxes on interest income and other exempt income received from U.S. sources by foreign intermediaries and providing a refund upon proof that the beneficial recipient was eligible. Avi-Yonah suggests this change with the hope that it would be adopted multilaterally.

A variation of this approach would be to require disclosure of the names of customers including beneficial owners, with withholding imposed if disclosure was not forthcoming. Such a proposal has been made by Michael McIntyre, and has been included, for accounts identified as U.S. beneficiaries in the HIRE Act, P.L. 111-147. The Stop Tax haven Abuse Act and President Obama's budget proposals addressed these issues as well. S. 3018, the Wyden-Gregg tax reform act, requires withholding on all accounts unless information on the beneficial owner is supplied, without an initial determination by the institute that the account has a U.S. owner.

President Obama's proposals also included some provisions to require information reporting by U.S. financial intermediaries and qualified intermediaries on transfers of funds and by U.S. persons and qualified intermediaries on the formation or acquisition of a foreign entity.

The proposed Stop Tax Haven Abuse Act would also require reporting by U.S. shareholders and persons forming, sending, or receiving assets from Passive Foreign Investment Corporations (PFICs), and this provision was included in the HIRE Act, P.L. 111-147.

Other Measures That Might Improve Compliance

Incentives/Sanctions for Tax Havens

Avi-Yonah and Avi-Yonah and Guttenberg suggest a carrot and stick approach to tax havens. They argue that little of the benefit of tax havens flows to their sometimes needy residents, but rather to the professionals providing banking and legal services, who often live elsewhere. They suggest transitional aid to move away from these offshore activities. For non-cooperating tax havens, they suggest the Treasury use its existing authority to deny benefits of the interest exemption. They suggest that tax havens cannot continue to exist unless the wealthy countries permit it, because funds are not productive in tax havens.

The proposed Stop Tax Haven Abuse Act would extend to tax enforcement the sanctions of the Patriot Act used to impose penalties for money laundering and terrorist financing. Sanctions vary in severity and range from increased reporting on transactions to prohibitions. Sullivan points out that the U.S. government has used the Patriot Act sparingly, however, and questions whether this change would be a credible threat.

Blessing suggests that sanctions should be multilateral rather than unilateral.

Revise and Strengthen the Qualified Intermediary (QI) Program

Several proposals relating to the QI program, which were discussed by witnesses at a Ways and Means Committee hearing on March 31, 2009, were reported by Sullivan. Some of these provisions are also included in the proposed Stop Tax Haven Abuse Act. If enough effective revisions could be made in the QI program, a great deal of potential information about U.S. taxpayers' income would be obtained. These proposals include the following. QIs would be required to inquire about and independently verify the ownership of foreign corporations and similar entities, information that they already must acquire to deal with money laundering. QIs would also be required to report any non-U.S. income of U.S. taxpayers. QIs would be required to submit information electronically, and IRS would be given resources to handle and use this information. The current exemption from withholding rules for bearer bonds (where no registration occurs) would be eliminated. Another possible change is to require QIs to share information about foreign customers to U.S. treaty partners (although one witness warned that this might be too severe a requirement). Finally, external audits of QIs would be strengthened by requiring QIs to promptly notify the IRS of any material failure in oversight, improve the evaluation of risk of circumvention of U.S. taxes by U.S. persons, and require audit oversight by a U.S. auditor.

Blum emphasizes the problem of accepting a shell corporation as the beneficial owner, and says this loophole in the law should be closed. He also suggests that penalties for failure to enforce should include withholding of capital gains as well as interest and dividends.

McIntyre stresses that audits of the QIs should be done by firms that do not at the same time sell tax shelters. Avi-Yonah and Avi-Yonah and Guttentag also suggest that IRS should require U.S. payors to issue form 1099s when they know or have reason to suspect the beneficial owner is a U.S. citizen (rather than the W8-BEN which provides evidence of foreign status).

President Obama's proposals would revise the treatment of non-qualified intermediaries. As noted above, the proposal includes a withholding/refund mechanism for non-qualified intermediaries. It would require that QIs can qualify only if all of their affiliates are QIs and, as noted above, increase information reporting by QIs.

The HIRE Act, P.L. 111-147, discussed below, contains some modifications in this area.

Placing the Burden of Proof on the Taxpayer

An important part of the Stop Tax Haven Abuse proposal is to place the burden of proof in court on the taxpayer; this approach was also suggested by Blum. As noted above, there is also a shift in the burden of proof for accounts with non-qualified intermediaries for filing an FBAR (Foreign Bank and Financial Account Report).

President Obama's proposal would create a presumption that the funds in foreign accounts are large enough to require an FBAR, which is required when amounts exceed $10,000. It would treat failure to file for amounts in excess of $200,000 as willful, which permits criminal penalties and larger civil penalties.

The HIRE Act (P.L. 111-147) would assume that, when adequate information is not provided, foreign accounts exceed the $50,000 minimum that requires reporting (under other provisions) on the tax return for purposes of assessing penalties.

Treat Shell Corporations as U.S. Firms

The Stop Tax Haven Abuse Act includes a provision to treat any firm that is publicly traded or has assets over $50 million as a U.S. corporation. This provision would include hedge funds but would not affect subsidiaries of multinational firms because decisions are made by the parent firm. Sullivan argues that such a provision would have a devastating effect on the U.S. hedge fund industry, where offshore firms generally attract tax exempt U.S. investors and foreigners who wish to avoid filing tax returns, as well as U.S. tax evaders, and that legislative relief for U.S. tax exempt investors (pension funds, university endowments) would be likely.

Impose Restrictions on Foreign Trusts

The proposed Stop Tax Haven Abuse Acts would impose further restrictions on foreign trusts, by providing that any powers held by trust protectors would be attributed to the trust grantor, providing that any U.S. person who benefits from the trust will be treated as a formal beneficiary even if not named, providing that a future or contingent beneficiary be treated as a current one, and treating loans of assets and property as distributions. The Senate Finance Committee draft would expand the definition of contributions to include items such as art and jewelry. The HIRE Act (P.L. 111-147) includes these provisions.

Treat Dividend Equivalents as Dividends

As noted earlier, the withholding tax on dividends has been avoided with the use of derivatives and other arrangements to re-characterize them as interest. The proposed Stop Tax Haven Abuse Act would treat dividend equivalents as dividends. Proposals for change in this area were also made by Avi-Yonah. President Obama's plan treats equity swaps as dividends. The HIRE Act (P.L. 111-147) includes this provision.

Extend the Statute of Limitations

Extensions in the statute of limitations are said by some to be needed due to the complexity of the international cases and difficulty of obtaining information. Extension has been proposed by numerous commentators, is supported by the IRS officials and is included in the proposed Stop Tax Haven Abuse Act, proposals discussed by the Senate Finance Committee, and proposals made by President Obama. These legislative proposals would extend the statute of limitations from 3 years to 6 years, but Blum also suggests the possibility of 10 years. The HIRE Act (P.L. 111-147) extends the statute of limitations to six years.

Greater Resources for the Internal Revenue Service to Focus on Offshore

Numerous suggestions have been made to expand IRS resources for combating overseas tax abuses. President Obama's proposal, for example, has proposed to fund 800 new positions to combat international abuses.

Blum says that agents should not be pressured to give up difficult cases because of short-term performance goals based on closing cases and collecting revenues.

Make Civil Cases Public as a Deterrent

Blum suggests all settlements involving offshore schemes in excess of $1 million should be excluded from the restrictions of Section 6103 that require settled civil cases to be confidential. He argues that no one knows about these cases and thus taxpayers think the possibility of being caught is small.

Revise Rules for FBAR (Foreign Bank Account Report)

Blum argues that language in the FBAR should be clarified to make it easier for the Justice Department to pursue cases; the proposed Stop Tax Haven Abuse Act would change the disclosure rules to make this information easier to use. The FBAR report on foreign bank accounts is filed separately from the tax return; individuals must check a box to indicate whether or not they have these accounts. It is possible that a reporting requirement on the tax return would increase the visibility and force of this requirement. The Senate Finance Committee would require this report to be filed with the tax return and require due diligence on the part of tax preparers to determine if it should be filed. (Note also, as discussed below, that some of the strengthened penalties relate to FBAR.) President Obama's FY2010 plan would require the information from the FBAR to also be reported on the tax return and any transfer of funds that sums to more than $10,000 would also be reported. His FY2011 plan increases the minimum to $50,000, and this provision is included in the HIRE Act (P.L. 111-147).

John Doe Summons

A provision in the proposed Stop Tax Haven Abuse Act would make it easier to issue John Doe summons where the IRS does not know the names of taxpayers and now must ask courts for permission to serve the summons. This section provides that in any case involving offshore secret accounts, the court is to presume tax compliance is at issue, to relieve the IRS of the obligation when the only records sought are U.S. bank records, and to issue John Doe summons for large investigative projects without addressing each set of summons separately.

Strengthening of Penalties

Increased penalties are included in the proposed Stop Tax Haven Abuse Act, the Finance Committee Draft and President Obama's proposals. Among the penalty provisions in various proposals are increased penalties for failure to file FBARs; basing the FBAR penalty on the highest amount in period rather than on a particular day; and increased penalties on abusive tax shelters, failure to file information on foreign trusts, and certain offshore transactions. President Obama's proposals would double accuracy-related penalties for foreign transactions and increase penalties for trusts and permit them to be imposed if the amount in the trust cannot be established; this provision was included in The HIRE Act (P.L. 111-147).

The proposed Stop Tax Haven Abuse Act also includes a provision that legal opinions that take the position that a transaction is more likely than not to prevail for tax purposes will no longer shield taxpayers from penalties.

S. 386, the Fraud Recovery and Investment Act, would introduce criminal penalties. Some tax attorneys have questioned whether these proposals are too harsh or might undermine amnesty or voluntary compliance.[96]

Address Tax Shelters; Codify Economic Substance Doctrine

The proposed Stop Tax Haven Abuse Act would make a number of additional changes addressing tax shelters, including prohibiting the patenting of tax shelters, developing an examination procedure so that bank regulators could detect questionable tax activities, disallowing fees contingent on tax savings, removing communication barriers between enforcement agencies, codifying regulations, making it clear that prohibition of disclosure by tax preparers does not prevent congressional subpoenas, and providing standards for tax shelter opinion letters.

It would also codify the economic substance doctrine. This proposal is discussed among options for reducing corporate tax avoidance, but would also be applicable to individual evasion issues. The health reform legislation (P.L. 111-148) codified the economic substance doctrine.

Regulate the Rules Used by States to Permit Incorporation

Blum suggests that all U.S. Limited Liability Companies (LLCs) have a taxpayer ID number, a requirement not imposed in Delaware and other states that keep no records of ownership. S. 569

---

[96] See Jeremiah Coder, "Proposed offshore Crime Legislation Worries Defense Bar," *Tax Notes Today*, March 23, 2009. The attorneys are concerned that money laundering charges would not have to be approved through the Department of Justice's tax division, that penalties of up to 20 years gives prosecutors too much power, that the provisions may trap taxpayers who want to participate in IRS voluntary disclosure, and that they would also discourage the "quiet disclosure" where taxpayers simply report past information.

would tighten regulations to require record-keeping and identification of beneficial owners of corporations and LLCs and commission a study of partnerships and trusts.

Make Suspicious Activity Reports Available to Civil Side of IRS

The proposal that information on suspicious activity reports filed by financial institutions under anti-money laundering acts be made available to the civil side of IRS was made by Blum, who indicated that agency policy at the top levels had prohibited this information sharing. It is included in a provision in the Stop Tax Haven Abuse Act.

Summary of Enacted Legislation

Two bills contain provisions relating to international compliance, the HIRE Act and the health reform legislation.

The Hiring Incentives to Restore Employment (HIRE) Act (P.L. 111-147)

The foreign provisions in this act are projected to have a relatively small effect, $8.7 billion over 10 years, when compared with estimated costs of international evasion of around $40 billion a year.

Reporting on Foreign Accounts

This provision would institute withholding on payments, at a 30% rate, to foreign financial institutions and other institutions unless certain requirements are met. Although the provision allows considerable regulatory scope, the requirements include providing specific details on U.S. beneficial owners. The institution determines U.S. beneficial owners, with oversight by the Treasury.

Deduction of Interest for Bearer (Non-Registered) Bonds

Non-registered bonds (with some exceptions, including those issued by natural persons, not for public sale, or of maturities of less than a year) are subject to restrictions, including an excise tax and denial of interest deductions; there is an exception for foreign targeted bonds. Foreign-targeted bonds are designed to be sold to non-U.S. persons, payable outside of the United States, and containing a statement that any bond held by a U.S. person will be subject to U.S. tax laws. This provision would repeal the foreign targeted bond exception for purposes of interest deductibility. Non-registered state and local bond interest for these bonds are also not eligible for tax exclusion.

Additional Information Reported on Tax Returns

Individuals who are required to file an FBAR (Foreign Bank and Financial Account Report) would also be required to report this information on the tax return if the amount in the account is $50,000 or more. For purposes of this report on the tax return, interests in foreign trusts would also be included. A presumption will be made that the amount of the account is at least $50,000 when no detailed information is provided.

Penalties

The 20% accuracy-related penalty that already applies would be increased to 40% for transactions involving foreign accounts where the taxpayer failed to disclose reportable information. A reasonable cause exception would not be available. In the case of failure to report or under-reporting foreign trusts, the initial penalty is 35% of the trust amount (5% in certain cases). If the failure to report continues for 90 days, an additional penalty of $10,000 is imposed for each 30-day period, but the total cannot exceed the amount of the trust. This provision would change the initial penalty from 35% (5%) of the trust amount a minimum of $10,000. The $10,000 for each 30-day period would be continued indefinitely, with a refund of any excess when the taxpayer does report. This proposal addresses the problem of the IRS not being able to assess a penalty because it cannot determine the amount in the account.

Statute of Limitations

The statute of limitations for cross-border transactions is extended from three to six years in instances where more than $5,000 of income is omitted.

Reporting on Foreign Passive Investment Companies

The legislation addresses reporting by passive foreign investment companies (PFICs) by codifying proposed regulations requiring shareholders to file annual information reports. The Secretary of the Treasury has regulatory authority over the type of information and can also provide for regulations that address duplicate reporting from other provisions in the legislation.

Electronic Filing

Electronic filing is required of persons who file at least 250 returns (including information returns). This legislation requires electronic filing for financial institutions regardless of whether the institution provides 250 returns, which would generally be relevant to foreign financial institutions.

Trusts

The legislation would further restrict foreign trusts by treating the grantor as the owner if there is a future contingency for a U.S. beneficiary or an agreement the grantor is involved in that might provide for a U.S. beneficiary. It also places the burden of proof on the grantor, treats a loan or use of property without appropriate compensation as a benefit, and requires information reporting.

Treat Equity Swaps as Dividends

This provision addresses the problem of disguising dividends that are subject to taxation as interest that is not. This provision, which would generally treat equity swaps as dividends, would raise $1.1 billion for FY2011-FY2020 according to the President's proposals.

Economic Substance Doctrine: The Patient Protection and Affordable Care Act, P.L. 111-148.

The health reform included the codification of the economic substance doctrine, requiring both a subjective (profit intended) and objective (profit achieved) test. This provision has been enacted as part of the revenue offsets and, although not specifically targeted to foreign transactions, would have a potential impact.

The Act: P.L. 111-226

On May 20, 2010, the Ways and Means Committee Chairman Levin and Senate Finance Committee Baucus released a plan for combining Senate and House proposals for extending temporary tax benefits and providing for spending increases.[97] Among the revenue raisers were several foreign provisions largely relating to the foreign tax credit, which were developed jointly with the Treasury Department. Some are also included in the President's 2011 budget proposals. They would raise $14.451 billion over 10 years. These provisions were adopted as part of H.R. 4213 on May 28, 2010.

Some of these issues arise from the overall limit on the foreign tax credit, which allows aggregate foreign taxes paid abroad to be credited against U.S. tax on aggregate foreign earnings. Under these rules, firms are either in excess credit positions (they have foreign taxes that cannot be used because aggregate foreign taxes exceed aggregate U.S. tax on foreign source income) or in an excess limit position (they don't have enough foreign taxes to offset U.S. tax on foreign source income). In the former case, any technique that increases the amount of their income that is considered foreign source reduces overall tax because it increases the limit on foreign tax credits; in the latter case, any technique that allows recognition of foreign taxes without the accompanying income reduces taxes.

H.R. 4213 was not enacted, but a smaller spending bill using H.R. 1586 as a vehicle included most of the foreign provisions in H.R. 4213. H.R. 1586 provided money to the states for education and Medicaid funding, with costs paid for in part by these foreign revisions. It was signed into law on August 10, 2010. The provisions are summarized below.

Preventing Splitting Foreign Tax Credits from Income

This provision would address the issue of reverse hybrids and mechanisms that allow firms to recognize and take credits for foreign taxes paid without reporting the income that gave rise to the foreign taxes (discussed earlier in this report), thus using those credits to offset tax on unrelated income. The proposal would implement a matching rule so that foreign tax credits would not be recognized until the income is taken into account. This proposal is estimated to raise $6.325 billion over 10 years.

---

[97] Press release at http://waysandmeans.house.gov/press/PRArticle.aspx?NewsID=11191; summary at http://waysandmeans.house.gov/media/pdf/111/America_Jobs_Summary.pdf.

Denial of Foreign Tax credits for Covered Asset Acquisitions

Taxpayers can acquire a firm by purchasing stock or by purchasing the underlying assets. In the latter case, assets are valued at current market value, which generally increases depreciation deductions. Certain U.S. tax rules allow a stock acquisition to be treated as an asset acquisition. Foreign governments may not apply a similar rule. As a result, depreciation deductions under the foreign rules are smaller than under the U.S. rules, and income and foreign taxes paid are higher. The excess of foreign taxes over U.S. taxes on this transaction can be used to offset U.S. tax on unrelated foreign income under the overall foreign tax credit limitation. Such an outcome can also occur when taxpayers acquire entities that are partnerships for U.S. purposes and corporations for foreign tax purposes. The proposal would prevent firms from obtaining credits for these excess taxes. This proposal is estimated to raise $4.025 billion over 10 years.

Separate Foreign Tax Credit Limit for Items Resourced Under Treaties

Current tax treaties provide that some income that would normally be considered U.S. source income can be resourced in foreign countries. For example, interest paid on U.S. securities to a firm's foreign subsidiary would normally be U.S. source income, but under a treaty may be sourced in the foreign country. The foreign country may tax net interest (interest income less interest paid), but the entire gross interest payment would be considered foreign source and eligible for offsetting foreign tax credits. This increase in foreign source income could, absent other provisions, lead to tax reductions from excess foreign taxes on other income. Current law places this operation in a separate foreign tax credit basket when the foreign firm is a subsidiary of a U.S. firm incorporated abroad. This provision extends the treatment to branch operations and disregarded entities (that are treated the same as branches under check the box rules). The provision would apply to taxable years beginning after the date of enactment. This proposal is estimated to raise $253 million over 10 years.

Limitation on the Use of Section 956 (the "Hopscotch" Rule)

The hopscotch rules issue arises from the combination of two different tax provisions. The first is the treatment of dividends from foreign subsidiaries when there are multiple tiers of these subsidiaries. For example, a U.S. parent might have a subsidiary (tier 1), which in turn has a subsidiary (tier 2). If a tier 2 firm wants to pay a dividend to the parent, it would first be paid to the tier 1 subsidiary, which would in turn pay it to the parent. The foreign tax credit allowed would be a blend of the tax rate in the tier one subsidiary and the tier 2 subsidiary. For example, if one-half of the income of the tier 1 subsidiary was its own and the tax rate was 10% and one-half was from the payment from the tier 2 firm with a 50% tax rate, and dividend paid by the tier 1 subsidiary to the U.S. parent would have a 30% rate. These deemed taxes paid could be used for foreign tax credits against any U.S. tax on foreign source income. The second provision is Section 956, which was designed to prevent firms from returning income to the U.S. parent without paying tax, but using methods such as lending to the parent or buying property from the parent. A payment made in this fashion is construed as a dividend. Therefore, if the tier 2 subsidiary made a transaction that fell into the Section 956 rules, it could "hopscotch" over the tier 1 subsidiary and receive a full 50% tax rate: two-thirds larger than the 30% rate allowed under the blended credit rule. This provision preserves the blended rate in the case of Section 956 transactions. This proposal is estimated to raise $1.010 billion over 10 years.

Special Rule for Certain Redemptions by Foreign Subsidiaries

This issue relates to circumstances where a foreign multinational company owns a U.S. firm, which in turn owns a foreign subsidiary, and the foreign subsidiary purchases stock in the U.S. firm from the foreign multinational with cash. The cash payment can be considered a direct dividend payment to the foreign multinational up to the earnings and profits of the foreign subsidiary and thus bypasses the U.S. tax system. (If earnings and profits of the subsidiary are exhausted the payment comes from earnings and profits of the U.S. company and are subject to dividend withholding taxes unless exempted by treaty.) The earnings and profits of the foreign subsidiary are reduced by the amount of the payment so that they are not available for future taxation. If the foreign subsidiary had paid a dividend directly to the U.S. parent, it would have been subject to tax at the firm level and to a withholding tax on the dividend (unless exempted by treaty). This provisions would not allow earnings and profits of the foreign subsidiary to be taken into account if more than 50% of the dividend would bypass the U.S. tax system. This proposal is estimated to raise $255 million over 10 years.

Modification of Affiliation Rules for Allocating Interest Expense

Foreign tax credits are limited to the U.S. tax that would be due on foreign source income if taxed in the United States. In determining foreign source income, a share of the interest paid by the U.S. parent and related U.S. affiliates is assigned to foreign income based on the share of total assets that are foreign. The more interest that is assigned to foreign sources, the smaller the foreign source income and the lower the foreign tax credit limit. Although the affiliate rules generally exclude foreign corporations, a special provision applies to foreign affiliates that are 80% owned and where 50% of earnings are effectively connected to U.S. business to prevent firms from hiding their interest in these types of affiliates. If the effectively connected earnings are greater than 80%, all interest and assets are taken into account. If the effectively connected earnings are between 50% and 80%, only the effectively connected assets and earnings are included. This provision provides that all assets and interest are included as long as effectively connected earnings are 50% or more. This proposal is estimated to raise $405 million over 10 years.

Repeal of 80/20 Rules

Under current law, dividends and interest paid by a domestic corporation are generally U.S. source income and subject to gross basis withholding if paid to a foreign person. (As discussed earlier in this report, portfolio interest and bank deposit interest paid to foreigners is exempt.) Interest and dividends paid by a firm with a least 80% of its gross income foreign source and due to an active foreign business are not subject to withholding. This interest can also increase foreign source income and the foreign tax credit limit. The determination of eligibility is made during the previous three-year period. The bill would repeal the 80/20 company rules (and also the 80/20 rules for resident alien individuals). The proposal would grandfather existing 80/20 companies if they also meet a new test (that combines the company with its existing subsidiaries) and if it does not add a new substantial line of business. It also excludes payment of interest on existing obligations. This provision is estimated to raise $153 million over 10 years.

Technical Correction to the HIRE Act

The bill would make a technical correction to the foreign compliance provisions of the Hiring Incentives to Restore Employment Act (P.L. 111-147) to clarify the statute of limitations.

Summary of Legislative Proposals

This section summarizes current legislative proposals that are designed to address or have consequences for international tax evasion and avoidance.

American Jobs and Closing Loopholes Act (H.R. 4213)

As noted above, most foreign provisions in H.R. 4213 were included in the act, P.L. 111-226. Below are two provisions, one specifically a foreign provision and one related to foreign tax issues, that were not included.

Source Rules on Guarantees

Dividends and interest are generally sourced depending on the residence of the payor, whereas payments for services are sourced to the country where the service is performed. The treatment of guarantee fees is unclear, depending on whether compared to interest or services. Sourcing these payments like services allows U.S. subsidiaries of foreign firms to make deductible payments that reduce U.S. income without paying the withholding tax (as they would with interest). This provision treats these fees the same as interest: sourced to the residence of the payor. Payments by foreign persons are also U.S. source if allocable to income effectively connected with U.S. business. Treasury is to identify other transactions that are in the nature of guarantees. This proposal is estimated to raise $2.025 billion over 10 years.

Boot-Within-Gain

The boot-within-gain revisions are generally applicable to domestic as well as foreign activities, but have implications for international transactions. When a person or firm sells stock and uses the proceeds to purchase other stocks, capital gain is recognized to the extent that the sales price of the stock exceeds the basis of that stock (typically what was originally paid for it). In general, a gain is not recognized in exchanges of stock in corporate reorganizations. If the exchange includes cash or property ("boot"), gain is recognized to the extent of the boot. If the boot is more than the gain, all of the boot will not be taxed. However, if the boot is considered equivalent to a dividend, it will be taxed in full. One of the rules that allows the payment not to be considered as a dividend is a termination of interest (liquidation). Check-the-box rules permit a transaction to be considered a liquidation for U.S. purposes (i.e., a disregarded entity), but not for foreign purposes. Thus one foreign subsidiary of a U.S. firm can pay cash to the U.S. parent for stock in another foreign subsidiary of the U.S. firm without the transactions being viewed as a dividend repatriation, thereby potentially reducing U.S. tax. In addition, two U.S. subsidiaries of a foreign parent can engage in a similar transaction without generated a U.S. withholding tax on the dividend. If the foreign parent does not have a treaty eliminating the tax, this treatment reduces U.S. taxes. This revision would treat payments in these cases as a dividend.

President Obama's International Tax Proposals[98]

President Obama's international proposals include several proposals that relate to multinational corporations: allocation of deductions and credits, a restriction on use of foreign tax credits when associated income is not recognized, and a restriction on check-the-box. They also include proposals addressing individual tax evasion. Overall these provisions are projected to raise $210 billion for FY2010-FY2019 as presented in the 2010 budget; $122 billion for FY2011-FY2020 as presented in the FY2011 budget; $129 billion for FY2012-FY2021 as presented in the FY2012 budget; and $148 billion for FY2013-FY2022 as presented in the FY2013 budget. The provisions are discussed in the order in which they are presented unless otherwise noted, since revenue effects depend on that order. Note also that the budget proposes additional resources for the IRS for international enforcement. In addition to budget proposals, President Obama presented a separate corporate tax reform proposal that included international provisions. This proposal included five elements: the allocation of interest for deferred income (discussed below), a tax on excess intangibles (discussed below), a minimum tax on foreign source income in low tax countries, disallowing a deduction for the cost of moving abroad, and providing a 20% credit for costs of moving an operation from abroad to the United States.[99]

Some of the President's proposals have been adopted. Two provisions relating to foreign tax credits were enacted in P.L. 111-226, and are noted. The HIRE Act (P.L. 111-147) included a provision treating equity swaps and other dividend equivalent payments as dividends; the other foreign compliance provisions were, in most cases, also in the President's FY2010 or FY2011 proposals. These provisions are not listed. The health reform legislation also included the economic substance doctrine which, although not specifically part of the international provisions in the budget proposals, is relevant to foreign enforcement.

The remainder of this section summarizes provisions in the budget proposals.

Provisions Affecting Multinational Corporations and Other Tax Law Changes

Hybrid Entities and Check-the Box

The most significant provision in the FY2010 budget, based on revenue gain, is a revision directed at hybrid entities and check-the-box. This provision requires that a corporation cannot disregard a subsidiary corporation unless it is incorporated in the same jurisdiction. This rule does not apply to the parent and its first level subsidiary. Thus, a U.S. parent with a subsidiary in a low tax country could treat that subsidiary as a branch (disregard it as a separate entity). The subsidiary in the low-tax country, however, could not treat its own high-tax country subsidiary as a disregarded entity. This provision was included in the FY2010 proposals, where it was projected to raise $86.5 billion for FY2010-FY2019.[100] It was not included in the FY2011 budget.

---

[98] These proposals are listed in the various Treasury Greenbooks, at http://www.treasury.gov/resource-center/tax-policy/Pages/general_explanation.aspx.

[99] *The President's Framework for Business Tax Reform: A Joint Report by the White House and the Department of the Treasury*, February 2012, http://www.treasury.gov/resource-center/tax-policy/Documents/The-Presidents-Framework-for-Business-Tax-Reform-02-22-2012.pdf.

[100] A discussion of these provisions and revenue estimates can be found in the Treasury's Green Book, General Explanations of the Administration's Fiscal Year 2010 Revenue Proposals, http://www.treas.gov/offices/tax-policy/ (continued...)

Allocation of Deductions and Credits

Two of these proposals would allocate deductions and credits, so as to deny those benefits until income is repatriated. This approach was included in a tax reform bill introduced by Chairman Rangel of the Ways and Means Committee in 2007 (H.R. 3970). A portion of overall deductions, such as interest, that reflect the share of foreign deferred income, would be disallowed until the income is repatriated. The foreign tax credit allocation rule would allow credits for the share of foreign taxes paid that is equal to the share of foreign source income repatriated, a provision the discussion of the proposals refers to as pooling. Disallowed deductions and credits would be carried forward. The proposal specifically excludes deductions for research and experimentation from the allocation rule. The FY2011 budget proposal was narrower, and it was limited to interest deductions; it also includes a different set of allocation rules.

The revenue gain for FY2009-FY2020 was $25.6 billion for the limit on interest deductions and $32.0 billion for the foreign tax credit pooling. The FY2010-FY2019 budget proposal was $60.1 billion for the deduction allocation and $24.5 billion for the foreign tax credit pooling in the FY2010 budget. These estimates were $37.7 billion and $52.4 billion for FY2011-FY2021 and $37.2 billion and $60.8 billion for FY2012-FY2022.

Limiting the Foreign Tax Credit; Reverse Hybrids (Enacted in P.L. 111-226)

Another provision aimed at multinational corporations would disallow foreign tax credits when the associated income is not received, as can occur with reverse hybrids. A matching rule would apply. This provision is estimated to raise $27.4 billion for FY2011-FY2020. (Note that a similar proposal was included in H.R. 4213, but was scored at only $6 billion.)

Taxing Excess Returns on Intangibles

This provision, which did not appear in the 2010 budget proposal, would treat excess returns in a low-tax country on intangibles transferred to it from the United States as Subpart F income (subject to current taxation) and in a separate foreign tax credit basket (so that other foreign taxes could not offset U.S. taxes due on the excess returns). This provision is most recently scored at $22.9 billion for FY2012-FY2022.

Transfer Pricing of Intangibles

The proposal would clarify several rules that are relevant to the transfer of intangibles. First, it would clarify that intangibles include workforce in place, goodwill, and going concern value. Second, it would allow the IRS commission to aggregate intangibles if that leads to a more appropriate value. Finally, it would clarify that intangibles are valued at their highest and best as it would be by a willing buyer and seller with reasonable knowledge of the relevant facts. This provision is projected to raise $1.6 billion for FY2012-FY2022.

(...continued)

library/grnbk09.pdf and General Explanations of the Administrations Fiscal Year 2011 Revenue Proposals, http://www.treas.gov/offices/tax-policy/library/greenbk10.pdf.

Disallow Deductions for Reinsurance Premiums to Foreign Affiliates

U.S. insurance companies can reduce taxes by purchasing reinsurance from foreign affiliates, with a deduction of the premiums by the U.S. firm but no tax on the income of the foreign affiliate. This provision would disallow these deductions for reinsurance premiums when they are more than 50% of the basic premiums received. This provision was not in the FY2010 budget; it is projected to raise $2.5 billion in revenue for 2012-2022.

Earnings Stripping by Inverted Firms

The proposal would apply the provisions on earnings stripping discussed in 2004 to inverted firms. For these firms the debt-to-equity safe harbor would be eliminated and non-guaranteed related party debt would not be deductible when debt exceeded the 25% threshold. Carry forwards of disallowed interest would be limited. This provision is projected to raise $4.4 billion for FY2012-FY2022. The FY2011 and later provisions appear broader than the FY2010 provision because it covers debt paid to unrelated parties but guaranteed by a related party.

Prevent Repatriation of Earnings in Cross-Border Transactions (Boot-Within Gain)

The plan includes a proposal to require that distributions that are characterized as reorganizations but are in the nature of a dividend repatriation are subject to tax. This issue arises within the framework of an exchange of stock on the one hand for stock and property (called "boot") and rules that provide the minimum of gain be based on the boot or overall gain. This proposal is projected to raise $297 million from FY2010 to FY2019. The 2011 budget includes a broader provision regarding to boot in gain that covers domestic transactions as well, and such a provision is also included in H.R. 4213.

Repeal 80/20 Rules (Enacted in P.L. 111-226)

This provision is related to dividends and affects individuals. Under current law, withholding is applied to interest and dividends paid by corporations, but there is an exception for firms who have 80% of their income from active foreign operations. This provision would repeal that exception, raising projected revenues of $1.2 billion for FY2011-FY2020.

Foreign Tax Credits for Dual Capacity Taxpayers

This provision would disallow a foreign tax credit for taxes paid where there is an income tax that is paid in part to receive a benefit (i.e., the firm is paying a tax in a dual capacity) unless the income tax is generally imposed on the country's own residents as well as foreign persons. The current rule does not require the tax to be imposed on the country's residents. This provision typically relates to taxes being substituted for royalties in oil producing countries; there is a provision that it will not abrogate any existing treaties. This provision was projected to raise $4.5 billion for FY2010-FY2019. The FY2011 and later budgets had a slightly different provision that restricts the tax credit to the amount that would be paid if the taxpayer were not a dual capacity taxpayer. The FY2012-FY2022 revenue gain was $10.7 billion.

Tax Gain on the Sale of a Partnership Interest on Look-through Basis

This provision, first appearing in the FY2013 budget outline, would require gain on sale of a partnership interest to be treated as income effectively connected to U.S. business (and thus taxable) to the extent of the transferor partner's effective connected income. It is projected to raise $2.6 billion for FY2012-FY2022.

Prevent Use of Leveraged Distributions from Foreign Related Corporations to Avoid Dividend Treatment

This provision, first appearing in the FY2013 budget outline, would address a mechanism to avoid treatment of a payment as a dividend (but rather a reduction in basis) when a foreign corporation funds the payment from a separate related foreign corporation. It is projected to raise $3.3 billion for FY2012-FY2022.

Extend Section 338(h)(16) to Certain Asset Acquisitions

This provision, first appearing in the FY2013 budget outline, extends rules limiting the ability of firms to increase foreign tax credits for certain asset acquisitions. It is estimated to raise $1 billion for FY2012-FY2022.

Remove Foreign Taxes from a Section 902 Corporation's Foreign Tax Credit Pool When Earnings Are Eliminated

This provision first appears in the FY2013 budget outline. Current law allows a foreign tax credit for dividends paid or deemed paid or certain transactions. This provision reduces foreign tax credits for any action that reduces earnings and profits, since a reduction in earnings and profits will ultimately reduce the potential amount of dividends. It is estimated at $0.4 billion for FY2012-FY2022.

Provisions Relating to Individual Tax Evasion, Not Enacted in the HIRE Act

The President's proposals included a number of provisions relating to individual evasion, including reporting of information, withholding, and various penalties. Overall these provisions were projected to raise revenues of $8.7 billion from FY2010 to FY2019 in the FY2010 budget and $5.4 billion from FY2011-FY2021 in the FY2011 budget. Most of these provisions, or some version of them, were adopted in the HIRE Act, including increased reporting on foreign accounts (withholding and information on U.S. beneficial owners). The remaining provisions are summarized below. These provisions were not in subsequent budgets.

Reporting on Transfers

U.S. persons' financial intermediaries and qualified intermediaries would be required to report financial transfers. U.S. persons and qualified intermediaries would be required to report the formation or establishment of a foreign entity. The floor is $10,000 in the FY2010 budget proposal, but $50,000 in the FY2011 proposal.

Additional Information Reported on Tax Returns: Lower Floor

The HIRE Act required individuals who are required to file an FBAR (Foreign Bank and Financial Account Reports) to report this information on the tax return if the amount in the account is $50,000 or more, a provision similar to the FY2011 budget proposal. The FY2010 proposal had a lower floor of $10,000.

Burden of Proof and Presumption Provisions

The FY2010 proposal contains a number of provisions that provide evidentiary presumptions (shifts in the burden of proof) in civil and administrative cases. If an individual has a foreign account it is presumed to be large enough to require filing an FBAR. If a person has an account of over $200,000 it is presumed that failure to file is willful (which opens the possibility of criminal as well as higher civil penalties). If a payment subject to withholding is made to a foreign person on an FDAP, the presumption is that that person is not eligible for withholding.

Statute of Limitation: No Floor

The statute of limitations for cross-border transactions is extended from three to six years with no floor in the FY2010 budget proposal; in the HIRE Act and the FY2011 budget, it applies to instances where more than $5,000 of income is omitted.

The Wyden-Gregg and Wyden Coats Tax Reform Bills

Major revisions to corporate international tax rules are also included in S. 3018, a general tax reform act introduced by Senators Wyden and Gregg in the 111th Congress, and a similar bill, S. 727, introduced by Senators Wyden and Coats in the 112th Congress.[101] As part of revenue to finance a lower tax rate, this bill eliminates deferral of tax on foreign source income (taxes income currently) which should largely eliminate any benefits of profit shifting, since income would be taxed in any case. It also imposes a per country foreign tax credit limit.

Chairman Camp's Territorial Tax Proposal and Senator Enzi's Bill (S. 2091)

These proposals would shift from the current system of deferral to a territorial tax, where no tax would be imposed on active dividends of foreign subsidiaries. Moving to a territorial tax increases the benefits for profit shifting to low-tax jurisdictions since there is never an issue of subsequent taxation, as is the case with deferral. The Camp proposal would combine a territorial tax with a lower corporate tax rate, while S. 2091 is a stand-along territorial tax provision. Both contain provisions to limit the scope of profit shifting, although it is not clear how effective they would be.[102]

---

[101] See "Obama Backs Corporate Tax Cut If Won't Raise Deficit," *Bloomberg*, January 25, 2011, http://www.bloomberg.com/news/2011-01-26/obama-backs-cut-in-u-s-corporate-tax-rate-only-if-it-won-t-affect-deficit.html.

[102] See CRS Report R42624, *Moving to a Territorial Income Tax: Options and Challenges*, by Jane G. Gravelle, for additional discussion.

The Camp proposal would limit the amount of borrowing by the U.S. parent, and would impose one of three anti-base-erosion options, two directed at intangible income. Option A is similar to a proposal made by President Obama in his budget proposals, that would tax excess earnings on intangibles (in excess of 150% of costs) in low tax jurisdictions as Subpart F. The inclusion would be phased out between a 10% and a 15% rate. Option B would tax income that is subject to an effective foreign tax rate below 10% unless it qualifies for a home country exception. The home country exception applies when a firm conducts an active trade or business in the home country, has a fixed place of business, and serves the local market. Option C would tax all foreign income from intangibles (whether earnings by the foreign subsidiary or royalty payments) but allow a deduction for 40%, resulting in a tax rate of 15% at a 25% statutory tax rate.

S. 2091 does not have provisions restricting borrowing. Its anti-base-erosion provisions are a version of Option B in the Camp proposal along with a version of the first part of Option C would be included. Income in countries with tax rates of half or less than the U.S. rate (17.5%) would be subject to tax. However, operations that conduct an active business, with employees and officers that contribute substantially, would be excepted except to the extent the income is intangible income of the CFC. The CFC's intangible income would be Subpart F income. These rules provide more scope for exemption as compared to the rules in the Discussion Draft which would require exempt income to carry out activities serving the home country market. The bill also includes the first part of Option C, allowing a 17.5% tax rate on intangible income (such as royalties) earned by a domestic corporation. Intangible income would be placed in a separate foreign tax credit basket.

Stop Tax Haven Abuse Act, S. 506 and H.R. 1265[103]

This bill has been introduced in the Senate by Senator Carl Levin and in the House by Representative Lloyd Doggett. As with the President's proposals, some of these provisions or related provisions in the bills introduced in the 111th Congress (S. 506 and H.R. 1245) were included in the HIRE Act. Provisions in the Stop Tax Haven Abuse that are addressed in the HIRE Act (P.L. 111-147) include burden of proof (Section 101), statute of limitations (Section 104), information reporting on U.S. beneficiaries of foreign accounts (Section 105), trust abuses (Section 106), treatment of dividend equivalents (Section 108), and PFICs (Section 109). Also, the health reform legislation included the economic substance doctrine. The original bill is summarized as introduced, including the provisions that have been enacted. Following that bill, the 112th Congress bill is summarized.

111th Congress (S. 506 and H.R. 1245)

Section 101 would provide a burden of proof change. It would require the taxpayer involved in offshore secrecy jurisdictions to produce evidence, based on the presumption that the taxpayer is in control, that funds or other property are not taxable income, and that the account is not large enough to trigger a reporting threshold. (The bill also addresses securities law issues.) This section also contains the list of 34 tax haven jurisdictions taken from IRS court filings, and

---

[103] For a more detailed explanation of the 111th Congress bill see Senator Levin's Introductory Remarks, March 3, 2009. This proposal has also been discussed by Martin Sullivan, "Proposals to Fight Offshore Tax Evasion, Part 3," *Tax Notes*, May 4, 2009, pp. 516-520. For a discussion of the 112th Congress bill see Senator Levin's Introductory Remarks, July 12, 2011.

provides Treasury with the authority to add or remove jurisdictions. An important standard for being excluded from the list is an effective, and automatic, exchange of information.

Section 102 would expand the provisions in the Patriot Act of 2001, which gave Treasury the authority to require domestic financial institutions to take special measures (including providing information and prohibiting transactions) with respect to foreign jurisdictions relating to money laundering to cover instances of impeding U.S. tax enforcement.

Section 103 would require a publicly traded corporation or one with gross assets of $50 million or more whose management and control occurs primarily in the United States to be treated as a U.S. company. This provision is directed at shell corporations, including hedge funds and investment management businesses, set up in jurisdictions such as the Cayman Islands. It would not apply to subsidiaries of U.S. corporations simply because some decisions are made at the parent headquarters, but would still apply to shell subsidiaries.

Section 104 would extend the limit on audit periods from three years to six years for offshore jurisdictions with secrecy laws.

Section 105 would require U.S. financial institutions and brokers to file 1099 forms for any foreign account when they know the beneficial owner is a U.S. person. It would also require these institutions to report to the IRS when they set up offshore accounts and entities.

Section 106 addresses potential trust abuses. Foreign trusts have employed liaisons called trust protectors as a way for shielding U.S. taxpayers exercising control over the trust; the legislation provides that any powers held by a trust protector would be attributed to the trust grantor. It also provides that any U.S. person benefitting from a trust is treated as a beneficiary even if not named in the trust instrument, that future or contingent beneficiaries are treated as current ones, and that loans of assets and property as well as cash or security are treated as trust distributions.

Section 107 addresses legal opinions, stating that an activity is more likely than not to survive challenge by the IRS, which are used to shield taxpayers from large penalties. The legislation provides that a legal opinion of this nature would not apply in an offshore secrecy jurisdiction, providing exceptions to protect legitimate operations.

Section 108 would prevent dividend equivalents from escaping the dividend withholding tax.

Section 109 addresses reporting by passive foreign investment corporations (PFICs) by codifying proposed regulations regarding PFIC reporting by direct or indirect shareholders who are U.S. persons, and also requiring reporting by U.S. persons who directly or indirectly cause the PFIC to be formed or sent or receive assets.

Some of the sections of title II of the bill affect securities law rather than tax issues. Some provisions are tax-related, however.

Section 204 addresses an IRS John Doe summons where the IRS does not know the names of taxpayers and now must ask courts for permission to serve the summons. This section provides that in any case involving offshore secret accounts, the court is to presume tax compliance is at issue, to relieve the IRS of the obligation when the only records sought are U.S. bank records, and to allow them to issue John Doe summonses for large investigative projects without addressing each set of summonses separately.

Section 205 would address issues relating to the Foreign Bank and Financial Account Report (FBAR) requirement for a person controlling a foreign financial account of over $10,000. This is an additional rule from the requirement to report this information on the tax return, and IRS is now charged with enforcing this FBAR requirement. This provision would amend tax disclosure rules to more easily permit IRS to use tax data, change the penalty to refer to the highest average in the account during a year (and not on a specific day), and allow IRS access to information on Suspicious Activity Reports (SAR).

The last title of the bill relates to abusive tax shelters, and contains several provisions. It would strengthen penalties, prohibit the patenting of tax shelters, require development of an examination procedure so that bank regulators could detect questionable tax activities, disallow fees contingent on tax savings for tax shelters, remove communication barriers between enforcement agencies, codify regulations and make it clear that prohibition of disclosure by tax preparers does not prevent congressional subpoenas, and provide standards for tax shelter opinion letters. It would also codify the economic substance doctrine, to require both an objective and subjective test for economic substance.

112th Congress (S. 1346 and H.R. 2669)

Section 101 would extend the sanctions for money laundering to impeding tax enforcement (similar to previous provision in Section 102).

Section 102 would strengthen and clarify FATCA (Foreign Account Tax Compliance Act, adopted as part of the HIRE Act) in a variety of ways, including additional burden of proof requirements, expand the types of accounts that need to be disclosed, and other revisions.

Section 103 is similar to Section 103 in the previous bill.

Section 104 is similar to Section 105 of the previous bill.

Section 105 would require credit default swap (CDS) payments sent from the United States to be sourced as U.S. income and subject to tax.

Section 106 would treat funds deposited in U.S. accounts as U.S. source income subject to tax.

Some of the sections in the next title do not relate to taxes. Those that do include

Section 201 would require multinational corporations to provide the Securities and Exchange Commission (SEC) with country by country information.

Section 202 would provide a penalty up to $1 million for hiding offshore stock holdings.

Section 205 is similar to Section 204 in the previous bill.

Section 206 is similar to Section 205 in the previous bill.

The final title of the bill relates to abusive tax shelters and is similar to provisions in the previous legislation.

Finance Committee Proposal, 111th Congress

A draft of this proposal was circulated on March 12, 2009, and has been discussed by Sullivan.[104] Several of its proposals were included in the HIRE Act (statute of limitations, requiring FBAR information to be filed with the tax return, increasing trust penalties to a minimum of $10,000, expanding the definition of distributions, and increasing the penalties for underpayments associated with foreign accounts).

- It would require entities transferring funds offshore to report to the IRS the amount, destination, and account information. Publicly traded companies would be excluded.

- The statute of limitations would be extended from three to six years for tax returns that report or should have reported certain international transactions.

- It would require the foreign bank and financial account report (FBAR) to be filed with the tax returns.

- Tax preparers would be required to ask due diligence questions to determine whether an FBAR should be filed.

- The foreign trust failure-to-file penalty would be increased to a $10,000 minimum and the definition of property considered to be a distribution for foreign trusts would be expanded, and would include artwork and jewelry.

- Fines and penalties on payments attributable to certain offshore transactions would be doubled.

- A provision in the Heroes Earnings Assistance and Relief Tax Act of 2008 (P.L. 110-245) would be modified to require offshore entities that hire workers under a government contract be treated as American employers by establishing a rule that any individual who performs at least 100 hours of service a month is an employee and not an independent contractor.

Fraud Enforcement and Recovery Act, S. 386, 111th Congress

This proposal, introduced by Chairman Leahy of the Senate Judiciary Committee, included a provision to apply the international money laundering statute to tax evasion, and set aside funds for the Justice Department to pursue financial fraud, including funds to the tax division. It had been passed by the Senate. The House version of the bill, H.R. 1748, and the enacted law, P.L. 111-21, did not include the tax provision but did include additional funds.

---

[104] See Committee on Finance News Release, March 12, 2009, http://finance.senate.gov/press/Bpress/2009press/prb031209b.pdf; See also Martin A. Sullivan, "Proposals to fight Offshore Tax Evasion, Part 2," *Tax Notes*, April 27, 2009, pp. 371-373.

Incorporation Transparency and Law Enforcement Assistance Act, S. 1483, H.R. 3416, 112th Congress

This proposal (introduced as S. 569 in the 111th Congress) would establish uniform requirements for states relating to the disclosure of beneficial owners of corporations and limited liability companies, including updating and maintenance of information after terminating, imposing additional requirements for those not U.S. citizens or permanent residents, providing penalties, and updating of such disclosures. It also authorizes a study of requirements of partnerships, trusts, and other legal entities. This bill is relevant, among other things, to issues raised about the use of states as international tax havens.

The Bipartisan Tax Fairness and Simplification Act

This general tax reform proposal introduced by Senators Wyden and Gregg in the 111th Congress (S. 3018) and Senators Wyden and Coats in the 112th Congress (S. 727) would, among other changes, lower the corporate tax rate from 35% to 24%. Among the base broadening provisions is a repeal of deferral and imposition of a per country foreign tax credit limit. The latter proposal would prevent cross-crediting across different countries. The bill also includes withholding on all foreign accounts, regardless of whether the account is considered by the foreign institution to have a U.S. beneficiary, unless there is full information reporting.

Author Contact Information

Jane G. Gravelle
Senior Specialist in Economic Policy
jgravelle@crs.loc.gov, 7-7829